*A Bright Sun & Long Shadows*
A candid reflection on the glorious and gruesome realities of creating a new life in France

Val J. Littman and Linda S. Korolewski

*A Bright Sun & Long Shadows*
ISBN: Softcover 978-1725510012
Copyright © 2017 by Val J. Littman and Linda S. Korolewski

All rights reserved. No part of this book may be reproduced or transmitted in any form or by any means, electronic or mechanical, including photocopying, recording, or by any information storage and retrieval system, without permission in writing from the publisher.

The author, has researched the quotations used in this book through individual online research and through a Publisher Licensing Service. If a copyright holder sees a failing to give proper credit or the use is not permitted under fair use practices, please contact the author at - allittman@gmail.com - to discuss possible future corrections.

To order additional copies of this book, contact:

Parson's Porch Books
1-423-475-7308
www.parsonsporch.com

Parson's Porch Books is an imprint of **Parson's Porch & Book Publishers** in Cleveland, Tennessee, which has double focus. We focus on the needs of creative writers who need a professional publisher to get their work to market, **&** we also focus on the needs of others by sharing our profits with those who struggle in poverty to meet their basic needs of food, clothing, shelter and safety.

*A Bright Sun & Long Shadows*

# Contents

Preface ............................................................................................ 7

Building a Dream ......................................................................... 11

    Of Beginnings, Endings, and Beginning Again ........................ 11
    Christmas 2000 ........................................................................ 13
    Bienvenue ................................................................................. 15
    A Lifeline ................................................................................. 17
    Uncertainty [3] ........................................................................ 22
    We move into *Cœur de Village* ............................................... 30
    Getting Settled ........................................................................ 36
    Halloween Approaches ........................................................... 41
    Louis Quatorze ....................................................................... 43
    Not yet a petit jardin ............................................................... 44
    The First Noël ........................................................................ 49
    Christmas 2001 ...................................................................... 50

Dreams and Nightmares – 2002 .................................................. 53

    The Everyday Face of France .................................................. 53
    Update from France – March ................................................. 56
    A Monday Morning ................................................................ 61
    The Kitchen Arrives ............................................................... 63
    Up-date from France – May .................................................... 66
    La Saison Commence ............................................................. 70
    Feux d'Artifice, François d'Assise and Folies Française ........... 74
    An Update from France – August ........................................... 76
    An update from France - Village Fête ..................................... 81
    September Scenes of Village Life ............................................ 83
    An Update from France – October/November ...................... 87
    An Acquired Taste .................................................................. 90
    Thanksgiving ........................................................................... 97
    Christmas 2002 ...................................................................... 98

Of Light and Shadow in 2003 .................................................................. 102

    A Heart Warming Experience ...................................................... 102
    An update from France – March .................................................. 105
    Doin' the Dustbin Shuffle ............................................................ 107
    An Update from France Spring .................................................... 111
    A basic law of physics: If it held wine, it will hold water ......... 114
    A Change of Focus ...................................................................... 123
    An Update from France – Autumn .............................................. 124
    Le petit jardin de l'âme ............................................................... 128

Epilogue ..................................................................................... 132

    Of Endings, Beginnings, and Endings ........................................ 132

Appendix .................................................................................... 135

Annotated Bibliography ............................................................. 147

# Preface

For my wife, Linda, and I, our early vacations to France were part vacation and part research in preparation for our retirement. When, at last, we purchased the village ruin we would someday call home, we took several "before" pictures. The early photos, like our vacations, had dual purposes. They documented the condition of the property and provided help in our planning. We used them to sketch the revisions, giving the builders the visual aide they needed to help us pull out of these old stones the inherent potential that we saw in them. But the unexpected, perhaps symbolic, purpose of our photographs was seen in the shadows. Our first pictures were marred often by deep shadows created by the angle and fierce brightness of the sun. Pictures of the front elevation of our village house were almost impossible. First, there was the narrowness of the street. We could not get a photo straight on, because we could not get the camera far enough away from the façade, even with our wide-angle lens. Secondly, there was the shadow cast by the sun. The sun, which highlighted the rustic beauty we wished to capture, also created deep shadows that obscured the architectural and structural detail. In time, we found photographic ways to overcome the shadows. But little did we know, that this was just the beginning of a way of life for us in France.

This is not the book I had intended to write. *A Bright Sun & Long Shadows* is a picture of life in France unlike the many we read during our years of preparation before we made the decision to retire to the Midi. In retrospect, our armchair research, our on-site preparatory vacations, and our personal contacts over a ten-year period heightened our anticipation about the best that France had to offer. We learned too little about the shady side of life in the Midi. Originally, the book I intended was of tales from our first year of adjustment to the new life in France. We expected culture shock and the stress that accompanies major life-changes – even when we so eagerly sought these changes for ourselves. The book, as originally envisioned, would have been like too many others. It would have chronicled our adjustments to French life. It would have reflected its charming curiosities with a little irony, and a lot of "looking at the bright side of things".

Yes, *A Bright Sun & Long Shadows* does reflect our experience of creating our new life in France. But, it has also grown beyond the initial intent; grown into a book that reflects how deeply the building of our new life has been affected by the dark side of French culture and the everyday ways of the people living around us.

As we tell our story, we hope, that indeed, you will see the charm of France, for France has much charm. She is the original *femme fatale*. On the sunny side, there are wonderful surprises and humorous tales of our new life's adventure. But, in this book I hope to show what others often overlook. The Shadow Side of life in France is less talked about, generally not printed, and yet affects every moment of life in France. This, we were not prepared for.

References to people and events, the humorous, and the sad ones, are from our experience of France. In most places, the names have been changed, but the events, even the most incredible, are real. This is not a scientific research sampling of the French and French customs. It is simply what we experienced. A categorical description of "The French" can be as misleading as any stereotype of any people. Many have tried this, still others have written to debunk such an over simplification. And the people of the Midi are often described as a unique people, even among the French themselves. It seems that the French, or any one culture defy convenient classifications.

I hope that you will find this book different in another way: I have tried to avoid the usual polemics found in many popular French-American, Anglo-French cross-culture books. I have tried to avoid the *"You must have misunderstood, that isn't what the French really mean"* approach. In our preparation to live in France we read many popular books from the genres of travel literature, living and working in France, cross-cultural adjustment, and some research oriented books on how best to handle the period of change to a new culture, as well as those on how one might attempt to explain French ways to foreigners. Now, in retrospect, I have found that, in illustrating a point, many cross-culture self-help books do not allow for the reality of a range of behaviors to be found on both sides of a cultural divide. Throughout our adjustment I often found that my own behavior did not resemble the "Americanisms" often characterized as brash, loud, and in-your-face. Nor did I find my French acquaintances the epitome of fashion flare, refinement, or diplomacy. So, I promise to avoid the usual dualism, of comparing base behaviors of one culture to the subtleties and finesse of another. Such convenient polarities and caricatures make for easy amusement, but put one or the other country's people in an artificial light. Instead, I present our experiences of the people we encountered and their behaviors as they affected us. Such a real-life sampling has a legitimacy of its own and its own special truth. No scientific sample can replace the experience of real life.

In writing this book I found myself tempted many times to digress into reflective analysis of one event or a group of events in which there seemed to be a pattern of behavior or some cultural significance. In the end, I have decided to tell the story first, and later, through an appendix, offer my reflection and analysis of a few trends that seemed to have significant impact on the creation and quality of our life in France. This way, whether you agree or disagree with my analysis, it will not interfere with the telling of our story. Read our story and come to your own conclusions.

Perhaps it is my theological and psychological background that made me comfortable long ago with looking at both sides of human life. It is the synthesis of both light and dark that creates this candid and reflective view of life in France. You will see that the approach in *A Bright Sun & Long Shadows* includes some differing views from both my wife and myself. Each of us, separately, having different views, of one experience. Perhaps it is a profound respect for Carl Jung that allows this look at the shadow side of life, as a part of life to be reckoned with rather than ignored. Perhaps at the end of your reading you will see that, at heart, Val is just an old curmudgeon and Linda an eternal optimist. Certainly, one risks a certain negative label by facing what is in the darkness. Yet, in the shadows lurks as much a reality as life in the sun.

One precautionary note: I make no pretense at speaking (or writing) perfect French. In some ways, the French phrases used throughout the book reflect our abilities at the time. We did our best to prepare, and we continue to learn, but if I were you, I wouldn't lean too heavily on the phrases you find here for use on your next vacation to France or in your "Learn French in Six Easy Lessons" class.

# Building a Dream
## 10% inspiration 90% perspiration

**Of Beginnings, Endings, and Beginning Again**

This book could have several beginning points. Our beginning as a couple could be a book of its own. Some have encouraged us to tell that story, of how we came together and created the chapters of our life from seminary and convent life, perhaps a "prequel" to the chapters of this book. Or perhaps we should begin with the evolution of our plan for retirement, a study in long term planning and discipline, productive goal setting and the realization of a dream. But for now, I've chosen to tell you a little bit about us as persons, and for now, it's the short version.

Our plans for retirement to France were not the first life change for us. In our lives, together, and separately, we both have negotiated major life changes. In our late 20's and early 30's we were among those professed Roman Catholic religious vocations that migrated to the secular world. We rebuilt our lives and established new professional identities. Each of us went on past our degrees in Theology to earn additional advanced degrees that fit us for work in the secular world. Together as a married couple we built up our life from a very modest one, into a successful and profitable one in corporate America. We found a new expression for our personal faith and grew new lives. In fact, these life changes, we felt, equipped us more for this next change in our life.

For better or for worse we are planners, inveterate professionals committed to setting goals, and reaching them. We approach our personal lives with much of the vigor that made us successful in our professional lives. Somewhere in our early 40s we began to seriously map out our retirement plans. We saved aggressively, researched assiduously, read voraciously, and consulted appropriately, all with a goal of financial independence and retirement at age 60.

As was our habit, we were ahead of plan. At age 53, we were ready to trade in our dual-career life-style. We had two full time jobs and a small B&B as a hobby. We were ready to sell our Victorian home and the years of careful renovation that it represented. We loved our Chicago urban life but were ready to make the move to rural France. We had purchased our property in France ten years earlier; a village ruin; no electricity, no plumbing, dirt floors. Over a period of ten years we had focused on structural necessities, as time and budget would allow.

After ten years, our some-day-it-would–be-a-B&B-in-France was far from complete. But, we were happy with the project and how our plan was evolving. Along the way, during our many work/vacations, we realized that it would be necessary to be on the spot, shoulder-to-shoulder with the workmen, to complete the project to our satisfaction. Someday, when the work was completed, our village ruin would be le petit jardin de l'âme, a small Chambres d'Hôtes with tastefully appointed rooms reflecting genteel country living. The name evolved out of the realization that the cultivation of this shared dream enriched our life together. It nourished our souls. We felt fortunate as a couple to have a common dream and the resources to make it happen. Our home at le petit jardin de l'âme was to be, for our guests, a place of reflection and restoration of the spirit in a simple, genteel rural setting. This was part of how we saw ourselves to be and what we wanted to share with others.

One year before our move to France, we purchased a smaller home I the same village. We were to live at *Cœur de Village* during the final phase of construction/renovation at le petit jardin de l'âme. After the renovation was complete and we were truly settled, we would rent this property – as supplemental income – when we no longer needed it as our "residence during construction".

Our Christmas letter to family and friends reflects the sentiments at the time of our departure from Chicago, our home, our professional lives, and the friendships that had grown over the past 20-plus years.

## Christmas 2000

For us, most of this year 2000 has been about "moving to France". And, at last, the long-awaited buyer for our home in Chicago has arrived. We have a contract and a closing date for February 28th. As I write this, we're putting together a very long "To-Do" list, so that we can take up residence in the south of France sometime in March 2001.

It was in late 1999 that we decided to speed up the timeline of our long-range planning. When we traveled to France in March of this year, we began the necessary steps to make our eventual move more immanent. The sale of our home in Chicago was the last necessary piece to accomplish our goal. Through the summer and fall, we lived in anticipation that, any day, the right buyer would come to our door. Over the Thanksgiving Holiday – after we'd settled in to accept the delay – it happened. We had two offers that same weekend. We've passed the crucial home inspection and attorneys' approvals and we're confident of the buyer's mortgage approval due in mid-January. I'll wait until the approval is secure before I announce my leave at Northern Trust. Linda has been making necessary business adjustments over the past several months.

To our friends we have been saying "good-byes" since last New Year. You've been patient with our ups and downs in this process of departure. We've also enjoyed the vicarious excitement of others as our dream takes on reality for them as well as ourselves. We've tried to prepare for the pains of adjusting to a new life and language, but, at this time, recognizing the inevitability of loss and frustration are mostly an intellectual exercise overshadowed by enthusiasm for what lies ahead.

To our families we've said good-bye. Linda's mother's side of the family had a reunion this summer, and it was a good time for both reunion and farewells. My parents joined us in France for vacation in September. We had great fun watching them enjoy their first trip to France. There are lots of nice memories, and we hope the starting point for their future trips.

Linda and I heartily recommend a significant uprooting every now and then. It is a sweet sadness to hear the good wishes of friends who both wish us well and wish we were not leaving just yet. Several of our dinners and many hugs have had that feeling of *"bon voyage"*, *"au revoir"* and often *"a bientôt"*.

The name of our new home – le petit jardin de l'âme - says something about our approach to life in general. It is good for the soul that we be uprooted now and again…transplanted, trimmed, and pruned. Twenty plus years ago, Linda and I each came to Chicago to grow a new life together. It's been hard work and wonderful. Now we're ready for the next great adventure in little garden of the soul.

Our new address in March will be:
Val J. Littman & Linda S. Korolewski
Le petit jardin de l'âme
10 Rue Molière
Florensac 34510 France

PS: We expect to be ready for our first B&B guests this summer. Check our web page for progress and eventually our phone and fax numbers.

Our last days in the USA were well planned in our usual efficient and thorough way. Notices given, transitions at work, the sale of our home, packers/movers/ dispatchers etc., all like clockwork. We left Chicago like two eager children off on a new adventure. We were successful adults mirroring what we believed, that anything is possible if you plan and work hard. We were a team; we had a dream and made it happen! We left Chicago happily married 23 years and looking forward to a grand celebration of our 25th anniversary in a new home with a new way of life!

Little did we know we were entering the land of both bright sun and long shadows.

## Bienvenue

We arrived in France March 03, to discover that our temporary home at *Cœur de Village* was not habitable.

To some degree, we had anticipated that the work would be behind schedule. The work had been originally scheduled for completion in time for our last vacation/ visit the previous September. At that time, it had been clear that workmen had not met the original September dead line, but surely, they would finish over the ensuing six months and it would be ready when we arrived in March. Promises made, work lists reviewed with the property manager and our follow-up done via Internet resulted in little change from September to March. The difference this time was that this was to be our home. Everything we owned – apart from two suitcases full of things to tide us over - was due to arrive in three weeks' time. We weren't ready. Le petit jardin de l'âme was officially still a ruin. And our temporary home was in ruins. We met this welcome to France as a challenge and set about to resolve the difficulties creatively.

Three weeks, in the south of France, passes like the "blink of an eye". There is a peculiar Mediterranean phenomenon, which I call the strobe light effect. Time moves along at a fixed, inevitable, pace; like clockwork, one might say. But workmen manage to move at a pace so incredibly slow that it produces an effect like a 1970's strobe light flashing on the dance floor of a disco. There is very little happening, but the allusion of movement fools the eye. Very little is accomplished and before you know it -- *voila*! Our personal property – all 292 boxes -- clothing wardrobes, antique furniture, art work, china and silver -- all those things we had carefully sorted and valued -- arrived from the USA promptly on schedule. Careful packing done in Chicago, under Linda's direction, was specifically labeled so that it could be delivered appropriately to either *Cœur de Village* (the house of our temporary residence) or *le petit jardin* (the larger and eventual residence). Neither place was in a suitable state to receive the delivery. More importantly, although our moving contract included insurance for a satisfactory delivery, there was no way to open these boxes to confirm their safe arrival. In preparation for the move, we had triaged our furniture and personal belongings, bringing only the most important, most valuable and most usable. The moving contract included placement, unpacking, set up and removal of the packaging. Not only was it impossible to unwrap the furniture, we decided that it was unwise to open and expose the carefully boxed contents to an undetermined period of construction traffic and debris. Antiques collected over twenty years and family heirlooms found temporary homes next to cement mixers, buckets of water, ropes and pulleys, dry wall and rusting bars of reinforcing steel. It would be four months before we could unpack the first of the boxes, and as much as two years later when we unpacked the last of box number 292.

Our good friends, who arrived one month after our arrival, expecting to help us paint and decorate *Cœur de Village*, took on that "can do attitude". We were nowhere near painting and decorating. Since we had no kitchen, we ate picnic breakfasts, picnic lunches, and picnic dinners. We worked daily next to the workmen -- when they showed up – and worked endlessly correcting errors and watch dogging their short cuts. We fired the property manager. Eventually, our friends returned to the USA from what had to have been a most unique vacation in France. We were much the better for their help, but nowhere near moving in to our temporary home.

Five months after our arrival in France, *Cœur de Village* was finished. Well, nearly finished. We moved in. We would complete the painting and decorating over the winter. Of course, during this delay, no work was being done on our primary project le petit jardin de l'âme.

During that first six months of life in France, we began to meet others who had embarked on the similar paths to create a new life in rural France. Painfully, we learned over and over that what we were experiencing in delays and quality of work was normal. This, our story, could have been the story of any one of the many who came to build their retirement dream in Mediterranean France. The quaint cultural idiosyncrasies and humorous tales, which we had read about prior to our move to France, had now come home to roost in a most unpleasant way. Our experience and what we now know is also the experience of many others, uncovered patterns of life for which we were not prepared.

> *Where light is brightest, shadows are deepest.*
> -Wolfgang Goethe

## A Lifeline

Sometime during the month of September, seven months after our arrival, we set up our computer on the third floor of *le petit jardin*, in the space that would someday be a home office. In this unfinished *grenier* / attic, under the protective cover of three layers of plastic sheeting, with an extension cord that traveled out the window of the *deuxième étage* / third floor down the front wall of the house and back into the garage (the closest room with electricity), we re-established a link to our past world. We had maintained essential correspondence during the summer by occasionally traveling to a Web Café in the nearby town of Pézenas. But at last, we would have some semblance of an office at home and a connection to the current century.

In some way, being "disconnected" from technology at this time, we were spared the full horror of the terrorist's bombing of the World Trade center. Since the events in NYC unfolded near the end of France's news day, our first information came in an old-fashioned way. Linda returned from the patisserie on the morning of 12 September saying, "Something must have happened, the town is a-buzz in little groups. I'm going to get a newspaper!" Even with our imperfect French we were able to read and re-read the news while the USA was in its second day of shock. For the entire week France continued to publish nothing but the news related to the terrorism and the aftermath. People from the village expressed their concern and inquired politely about our families and friends. We felt a bit exposed as the only Americans in the village, easily recognized by even the most casual observer. At the same time, we felt safe to be in small town rural France far from the maddening crowds. Because of the lack of television, we were protected from re-living the event via unrelenting journalism flashbacks and fast breaking news briefings. Our intake of information in the aftermath was kept current, but modified and modulated, by the daily press and a few moments at the computer keeping in touch with friends in the USA from our construction site in the south of France. The stark contrast of our new life against that of our family and friends across the Atlantic was more apparent than we could have ever imagined.

Email exchanges with dear friends and former colleagues were also a way of keeping our sanity during the serious, upheaval that we were experiencing. Such correspondence kept the remembrance alive of a time of life when I was once a competent professional. Here in our new land, with a new language and new values, the feeling of competence and confidence was being eroded.

Correspondence like the following was a breath of life, helping to reinforce how fortunate I was, and was perceived to be, in the eyes of those left behind at the workplace.

>Date: 2001
>
>Subject: good to hear from you.
>
>Val,
>
>How good to hear from you? Your electronic postcard is very welcome during these times -- again it refuels my ability to live through someone else for a few minutes. Haven't I told you at least 37 times that you picked a great time to get the heck out of this goofy business? Now I'm torn between (a) the righteous thought that you reaped the harvest of all the good you did in your life, or the dark (b) Val & Linda were really CIA operatives who knew the craziness was about to begin and flew to safety in the South of France. Whaddaya like, spiritual-karma books or spy thrillers?

In particular, I enjoyed the email "banter" with former colleagues. It was mostly true. That is, it was our presentation to the world of our family and friends of the brightest and most humorous side of our new life. It also became a way for me to listen to myself as I interpreted our new life around us.

Date: 2001
Subject: Response to Dan.

Sorry I will not be able to attend the breakfast meeting of the Bank Employee Assistance Professionals, but I'll think of you all and toast you with a croissant on Wednesday morning.

Regarding an interpretation of the timing of our "get away"; I choose the Spiritual Karma approach - I know I could not work for the CIA. I must say there are many moments when I feel like we made our move just at the right time. I think "luck" has more to do with our move and the timing than any reward for a good life. Lots of planning and luck – but "good Karma" is a nice thought.

Although our stock portfolio has suffered the same as everyone else, we both realize that if we were not already here, we would be delaying the move indefinitely. As it is, we are here, and we will deal with it. Luckily our plans included not having to draw on income from our long-term investments for two years. Hopefully, that will allow for some recovery.

I forgot to mention two south of France stories for your Employee Assistance Professionals (EAP) annals. We were making great progress on the renovation recently. At last we seemed to have mastered getting workmen that show up on time. We found a plasterer who was doing great work. Many of the walls in our house will be old time real plaster rather than plaster board. The plastering is a special skill and physically very demanding. Last week our plasterer told us he had to go to Avignon to settle an old court matter. Well, it seems that now our plasterer is in prison. Talk in the village has it that he loaned his car (uninsured) to his ex-wife who was in an auto accident and killed someone. He's in big trouble and we will not be seeing him for a long time. This morning our property manager showed up but looked like his face was run over by a truck! Several stitches and cuts and bruises it seems were the result of his being attacked by a *gitan* (gypsy) as he was coming out of the bar late last night. He says he did nothing to provoke the attack. Technically, there's no work problem since he showed up this morning and did put in a full day. But, I thought I would ask my former colleagues in the Employee Assistance Professionals group for their collective wisdom on how to handle gypsy related attacks on employees!

Val

Dan decided to comment on the comic hopelessness conveyed in my email.

Date: 2001
Subject: A Response from the SJL

A MESSAGE FROM THE ST. JUDE LEAGUE OF CHICAGO

Dear Mr. Littman,

We have received your petition for aid and have taken the matter before our international evaluation committee to determine whether yours is indeed a hopeless case. Unfortunately, Monsieurs LaRocque and Thibault are presently away on holiday. They are expected back sometime next week or the next. Let me assure you that upon their return we will schedule a meeting to consider placing your request before our most holy patron. In the meantime, we wish you well and encourage you to visit any of our shrines.

Yours in Hopelessness, Dan

Val's response to Dan's email follows:

Dear SJL customer services,
I am sorry to hear that Monsieurs LaRocque and Thibault are away on holiday just when I needed them most. Since

the SJL was not able to help me, I made my plea through the Episcopal Church. They were very responsive and effective. The Episcopal Church put me directly in touch with a group called AA (Angels and Archangels). They wished to remain anonymous.

I am disappointed that SJL was not able to help me, but I am no longer hopeless.

Patiently yours,
Val J. Littman

Some weeks later, after Dan's SJL email there appeared in our mail slot the following photocopied prayer to St. Rita. I decided to send this prayer to my friend with the following short note:

Date: 2001

Subject: SJL

Dear Dan,

Since you seem to be my "contact person" for the local Saint Jude League, I thought you would be interested in this little "Prayer to St. Rita of the Impossible".

We received this little gem stuffed into our b*oite de letters* / mailbox; perhaps from some devout Roman Catholic neighbor, perhaps someone who wants to give me an update on saints dedicated to impossible causes! Perhaps there was a need in France to "cross train" the saints due to the increased demand for help in impossible cases in France... an attempt to take some of the burden from St. Jude

Whatever the case, I thought of you.

Take Care

Val

P.S. My French is still rather basic. But, from the bold printed heading of the prayer it is not clear to me whether

St. Rita is to be prayed to <u>for</u> impossible causes -or- whether St. Rita of the impossible, <u>is</u> <u>herself</u>, impossible.

---

**Prière à Sainte Rita de l'impossible**

**Oh, ma glorieuse Sainte Rita de l'impossible !
Vous qui connaissez mon Cœur angoisse
Intercédez auprès du père pour moi**

## *Demandez-lui de m'accorder la grâce*

**(Lui demander ce dont on a besoin)
Je vous Glorifie et je vous Glorifierai
Je vous loue et je vous louerai pour toujours
Je me prosterne devant vous**

*(à ce moment dire un Notre Père un Je vous Salue Marie, et deux Gloire Au Père, trois fois)*

*Attention, celui qui trouve cette et désire en bénéficier, doit en faire 25 copies et les déposer dans une église pour les diffuser. Sa grâce sera exaucée aussi difficile soit-elle.*

*Prière : Je crois en Dieu de toutes mes forces et je demande à Dieu d'éclairer mon chemin et ma vie. Avertissement Après la distribution des 25 copies. Observez ce qui se passe le 4ᵉ jour
Une fois la grâce reçue, ressentez et montre de la gratitude*

---

**Uncertainty** [3]

Correspondence with friends from our past life, helpful as they were, could not begin to reflect the gradual erosion of our energies, and our honeymoon period in France. Nearly six months after we had said our good byes in the USA, we were still living out of a suitcase and not yet settled into our temporary home at *Cœur de Village*.

Years of preparatory language courses had not prepared us for the accent of the Midi and the Languedoc. When we arrived in France, we had some confidence that we were prepared for the basics of everyday French conversation. We were under no allusions of speaking fluent French; but certainly, we could do our grocery shopping, pay our bills and share the common everyday pleasantries necessary for village life. We were well read in how vocabulary and pronunciation were regulated by the *L'Académie française*. We knew of the pride the French take in their language. The reputation that the French have for resisting use of other languages is nearly as well-known as that of Americans' reluctance to learn a second language. But our experience of everyday French quickly deflated any confidence we had. Our ears, searching for familiar sounds were dumbfounded. Well-intended locals corrected even the simplest phrases of which we were once confident. "*Une Baguette*", certainly Linda could correctly ask for a simple baguette at the Boulangerie. No, it's "un-<u>neh</u> Ba-guet-<u>teh</u>", each syllable was pounced on mercilessly. I found myself staring blankly at the 80-year-old lady, selling vegetables, as she told me the cost of my purchase – "Diz-zeh nuf-feh". In my head behind the blank look, I asked myself, "What's a *Nuffeh*". It all became embarrassingly clear as she pointed to the total on the ticket. "*Dix-neuf*", of course, I know "*dix-neuf*", but I had not been prepared for those extra syllables. French in the Languedoc seems to have more in common with its Mediterranean neighbors in Italy and Spain. Clearly, in the Midi, we were far away from the influence of L'Académie française and Parisian standards for pronunciation. There was plenty of pride in the local dialect, but it often had little or no resemblance to the French we learned. Most important for our adjustment to life in France, the idiosyncrasies of the Langue d'Oc of the Midi had a disabling effect, casting doubt on our abilities rather than encouraging progress.

Such "midi-isms" were compounded by my own faux pas. It became difficult to tell if the quizzical look on the face of our French neighbors was due to an error in grammar, syntax, pronunciation, or some *lapsus mentis linguae gallicae*. As I tried to discuss my personal preference for wine aged in oak, did I say *"Elevé en fûts de chêne"*? Or did I pronounce it incorrectly, saying *chien (dog)* when I clearly meant *chêne* (oak)? As an anecdote of life in France these may, at first, seem quaint. But confidence fades, frustration grows, and one finds oneself silenced when every sentence must be weighed, mentally practiced, and then corrected after it dares to be spoken. Nothing could be done by habit – our habits were in English and from another way of life.

Uncertainty about out language skills led to some complicated, not to mention embarrassing, social scenarios. One day, only a few weeks after our arrival, as I was working at *Cœur de Village*, a woman about my age approached the door. She introduced herself as Madame Dupont. The name was familiar to me, since in the interest of building relationships with our future neighbors, we had in recent years exchanged Christmas greeting cards and simple correspondence. While taking our vacations before moving to France, we had met briefly first one and then another of the neighbors who lived near the ruin we would someday call le petit jardin de l'âme. We had discovered that a Monsieur Dupont owned a *grange* (a barn turned garage) adjacent to our property. We had made an inquiry about purchasing it. While the offer had been refused, it began a friendly exchange, and on another vacation encounter, Monsieur Dupont had helped us fix a flat tire on our rental car.

Madame Dupont, now standing at the door, confirmed that I was indeed the American who purchased the property adjacent to their garage. Then she began to tell me that Monsieur Dupont had died earlier in the year not long before our arrival. Clearly, she was still grieving. As tears began to well in her eyes, I searched my brain for appropriate French expressions of condolence and we spoke for a few minutes about the time and circumstances of his death. Nearing the end of our conversation, she raised the issue of the garage, and asked if we were still interested. Restraining my enthusiasm, I said, yes. She then went on to explain that she had a 12-year-old son who by French law must be considered in any sale of the property, if it were to be sold. We said our good-byes knowing that we would meet again.

That night I searched our trusty *Oxford Hachette French-English Dictionary* for sample *lettres condoléances*. I hand delivered my note the next morning, dropping it into the Dupont letterbox, feeling proud of my social etiquette française.

Later that same day on rue Molière, while Linda and I were getting into our car... an apparition?  Here comes Monsieur Dupont, down the street, a healthy looking 60-something riding his bicycle, just as we had remembered him from our last vacation. Fundamentals of conversational French aside, what does one say to the recently deceased?  *"Bon jour!"*  Our amazement was hard to contain, but we were not up to the task of creating, in French, the socially correct phrase with perhaps just the right amount of wit. "How nice to see you, Monsieur Dupont! I see that rumors of your death were gravely exaggerated...etc."  So, we muddled through simple hellos and comments about the weather and to our relief, a good-bye. We stared at each other in utter disbelief and realized that never was there a chapter like this one in our "Learn French in Six Easy Lessons" books. I spent the afternoon mentally sorting through that previous conversation with the Widow Dupont. Could my French be so, so off base?  Did I really misunderstand so badly?  Now, just how do I recover gracefully and approach Madame Dupont?

To retrieve my foot out of my mouth, I made the socially awkward return trip to explain my faux pas to Madame Dupont. Rehearsing my opening lines in my head, I rang the doorbell. She appeared at the doorway and motioned me into the courtyard.

*"Je crois, Madame, que j'ai fait une grande faux pas"* (I believe, madame, that I have made a grand faux pas.)

She looked puzzled.

Okay?  Now, is she puzzled because I have an incorrect sentence, or is she puzzled in the same way that I am puzzled?  I explained, in short simple sentences, that yesterday she told me her husband had died. Correct?

"Yes."

Ahh, green light, go ahead. I continued as best my French would allow.

"This afternoon, the man we know as Monsieur Dupont was riding his bicycle on rue Molière, and we said hello."

"Correct, yes." Ooh, now I _am_ confused.

Madame came to the rescue. The man we had seen was indeed Monsieur Dupont, her father-in-law. He is strong-as-an-ox, very fit and looks younger than his 80 years. The younger Monsieur Dupont, a man we never had met, but to whom we had apparently been sending Christmas cards every year, her husband, had died. She reassured me that I had not misunderstood, and thanked me for the *lettre de condoléance*. We gave a hug – an American kind of hug – it just seemed natural; she was thanking me for my effort, and I was just so relieved.

In some ways this event proved an ice-breaker for future social interactions. But, wouldn't it all be made easier if we used first names in our conversations?

This points out another social idiosyncrasy. The absence of personal names in everyday conversation adds to social uncertainty in France.

Our personal acquaintances and professional social contacts in the United States included an introduction by name with the shake of a hand, and often for social security, a repetition of that name during the conversation and again at the point of saying farewell. Many times, there was an exchange of a personal card or business card that included the name and more.

We found ourselves in our new land, introducing ourselves, but without a reciprocal introduction by name. The entire conversation, from *"Bon jour"* to *"Au revoir, a bientôt",* was completed without knowing to whom we were speaking. Linda and I began identifying people by their memorable characteristics. The cast of characters from the village came to include Madame Spiky-hair, Monsieur and Madame Handsome-son, Madame Blonde, Monsieur Four-kisses, Monsieur Hot Chestnuts, and a family, that to this day, we affectionately call "The Bundys" – after the T.V. sitcom "Married with Children". There were, by contrast, a few people who did introduce themselves and even encouraged us to call them by their first names. These few were, and by their own personal style, more outgoing. But the norm was for people to remain anonymous. If we were lucky, over time, we could pick up names, usually from a reference made by a third party during conversation, but then, we felt unsure if we could use it to address the person directly. Various commentators on the ways of life in France identify this characteristic as the French penchant for privacy. Knowing a person by name seems a connotation of intimacy that must be earned. The result is to leave the foreigner truly lost, without a future personal frame-of-reference for conducting the commerce of everyday life. It becomes difficult to invite someone for an aperitif without a name. Or send a thank you note for a little kindness done, or even to catch someone's attention at the market when they have left something behind, or, in the case of the Dupont family, to know which Monsieur Dupont had died. Often, the lack of a name results in creating a social and emotional position like that of a child to an adult. How many times while trying to make conversation was I reduced to referring to the man (or woman) "who lives in the house with the blue door", or "the person who has the big dog". People can be quite congenial in their anonymity, but there is a clear delineation between those who know and those who do not. It leaves one always off balance, uncertain, an outsider.

Not all our encounters, anonymous or otherwise were so benign.

Being at the work site of *Cœur de Village*, during our first three months in France raised our concerns about the quality of some of the work, how the subcontracting was being handled, and how the project in general was being managed. In additional to the fact that, we were painfully aware that the project was seriously behind schedule, we had questions about decisions that were made related to the plumbing and ventilation. At first, we tentatively questioned practices that we perceived as unusual. We found that we risked alienating ourselves from our primary link to the construction process. We had been told of how people in the past had been "black-listed"; rumors spread to discredit them and the wily ways in which "the scores" get settled in the south. Now it was becoming clear why we had been told these stories.

We feared reprisal. Until now, stories of herbicides "accidentally" sprayed on a row of bushes that obstructed another's view, and evacuation drains "accidentally" blocked by an irate workman seemed to us to be just so much braggadocio. Two stories of toilets that flushed into nowhere seemed incredible. Rumors spread about debits owed, or financial solvency affected a person's ability to do business whether they were true or not. And there had been talk in the market place of fires set to the property of Independent Vignerons by those loyal to the Cave Cooperatives. This was a part of life in the Midi, a form of primitive vigilante justice. It conjured up images of *Jean De Florette* and *Manon Of the Spring*. These stories made the fear of reprisal very real to us. Eventually, we addressed what seemed to us to be mismanagement and took the risk of the confrontation, but not without sleepless nights.

Linda writes in our journal:

> Saturday, in the early morning hours ...I woke up troubled, that someone was breaking into our house. These nightly awakenings are usually troubled, not knowing who to trust. Right now, I could use a little rejuvenation. I need to hold our goal before me to keep sight of the prize. I look forward to falling into a quieter spirit. But maybe what I need to do is to be quiet and at peace in the face of this disquieting time. As I write this I realize that if we are to provide a place of peace and rejuvenation we need to practice it here and now under these circumstances. ...

I write:

> I am finding it difficult to be so unsettled for so long, perhaps it is the state of "living out of a suitcase". Perhaps it is my perennial problem of focusing on the task rather than the process. But now after our very unpleasant encounter today with the project manager, I believe that I have a better sense of what has me "off kilter – off

center". I am more aware of the energy taken - used up unproductively - by this relationship. On the surface, the effort it takes to correct errors, oversights, miscommunications, and just plain shoddy workmanship was obvious to me. In the absence of a better alternative, I tolerated this unsatisfactory relationship. But in today's confrontation it became clear that we have let ourselves be used. About myself I learned - or rather, was reminded of – a lesson in surrendering in the face of evil. I would and still am more likely to rise to the challenge of some injustice rather than to yield and move out of harm's way. Your comment's, my love, were so on target. They remind me of Scott Peck's *People of The Lie*. I believe we took a step today to move out of harm's way, to let it pass over, rather than to use any more valuable time and energy. Still, I have difficulty in yielding, but maybe tomorrow I will be one day more mature to surrender rather than to challenge the lie that comes to steal away my life – or the life I came to Franc to live.

We had that horrible sinking "David meets Goliath" feeling that comes with the realization that we had confronted an injustice that was bigger than ourselves. We risked a future shaped by rumors spread about us by the disgruntled. Here in this land we had no personal history that served as a defense of our good name. We were foreigners – strangers - whose history could be fabricated at will. For months, I carried in my wallet a bill marked "paid" to counter rumors of non-payment from one workman. It was my security blanket.

This first summer in France brought us in touch with a lifestyle darker than any to which we were accustomed. More importantly, we were painfully aware of our own powerlessness. Being frustrated by limited language skills and surrounded by questionable business practices was difficult. But, most difficult of all was the loss of our personal professional context to support our integrity. Linda described it as a loss of our moral community. We were alone, and it was frightening.

Val J Littman and Linda S. Korolewski

## We move into *Cœur de Village*

Eventually and tentatively, side-stepping paint cans, ladders and assorted renovation materials in what was later referred to as the "Entry Salon", we moved into *Cœur de Village*, our temporary home. There was still much by way of decorating to be done, but after five months, it was a relief to unpack our suitcases, have breakfast coffee in our kitchen, and re-establish some of the basic rituals of daily life. The move to our temporary home at *Cœur de Village* proved to be a mixed blessing. The entries in our journal show a marked difference in view.

I write:

> The good news is we moved, at last, into our temporary home at *Cœur de Village*, the bad news is …we moved into *Cœur de Village*! It is a wonderful little house. I am really pleased with our renovations. A few unfinished tasks remain, but it has taken shape nicely. It is very charming. The bad news is, it is surrounded by non-stop ambient noise. I feel that I've moved into the projects. I can overlook the renovation noise from next door – after all, we have created our share in the past and it is temporary. But the "ghetto blaster" across the street makes me think that we have been transported to an Arabian Souk. We are treated, nearly every morning, to two hours of what at first seems like an Islamic call to prayer. This escalates into tribal-like cries and dance. In the evening we have a reprise, slightly more subdued. Being summer, the children in groups of 8-10 or more play. Picturesque narrow village streets, not more than two meters wide, become an every-day playground, football field or bicycle crash course for children ranging from around two years of age to pre-teens. Each day begins with happy little sounds and accelerates to screams and tears, interrupted at regular intervals with the predictable, but long overdue intervention of a parent shouting to be heard above the chaos. I don't want to become a grumpy old man seeming to be intolerant to the joyful sounds of children. That's not it. It is the endlessness that drives me mad. We have a

short truce around lunchtime until parents send the children back to the street. And a reprieve at dinnertime until the adults join the children with animated conversation, ball playing, and banter until midnight. At last near midnight, we approach the tranquility I expected of rural village life. On some nights, this too is shattered by the sounds of the neighborhood bar cranking up its sound system, pulsing its way into my sleep until I am reluctantly drawn back into consciousness at 1:00am.

Linda writes to a friend:

Hi Ann,

My life here; I'm loving it here. I can't believe how much it suits me. But, even after several months, I find that I must relax my shoulders. I tend to tense them all the time – e.g. when I step to the sink to brush my teeth or do the dishes, I am like a runner at-the-ready waiting for the gun to go off at the start of a race.

I've had a relaxing morning.... Each day I go for a long walk around the village. There's a levee for flood control that's perfect for a walk, where I see the horses, donkey, chickens, etc., that live in the village, as well as the farmers driving their tractors to and from the vineyards. It's like going home for me. I love the sun and the wind on my face and the view of the weather as it comes across the country – something I couldn't see in Chicago with all the buildings.

I'm *très content*. My big challenge is Val. How can two people have such different reactions to the same life events.... For example, we were having lunch, and something happened outside. He exploded "F..." I thought, "What in the world?" Of course, it had nothing to do with me – something outside, like the Moroccan music -- but it's like being shot, or having to run for shelter.... I feel like I'm in a smoke-filled room and want to get out. I'll appreciate any insights on how to deal with such an environment...

Our personal journal entries do not reveal one shared but unspoken disappointment. When we first purchased the house known here, as *Cœur de Village*. The name of our home was to be called *Niche Tranquille*. The name was to reflect the little niches we uncovered in our renovation and the place of tranquility, which this home once enjoyed as part of the 16th century protestant temple. The historic marker was placed just outside our front door. We anticipated pleasant morning sounds and the quiet bustle of everyday village life in rural France. After living in *Niche Tranquille* for a few months, it was clear that the name must change. We had, unfortunately, settled on a street that boasts of 30 primary school age children, and a way of life that was hundreds of decibels above my expectations. *Cœur de Village* was a name we could live with: it was both honest to its environment and, we hoped, not too off-putting when the time came, later, to rent the property. Clearly, a tranquil niche it was not.

A frequent conversation piece, we discovered, among foreigners is the choice to live in a village or in the countryside. People who live in the countryside value the open space and privacy, but often they express their fear of being alone, vulnerable to "things that go bump in the night", strangers passing by and theft when they themselves are absent from the house with no one near enough to see or to hear the actions of burglary underway. We, too did the "pros and cons" of village life versus countryside as part of our research before purchasing our properties. We chose life in the village because we expected to grow old in our retirement in France. We wanted social interaction rather than the isolation that seemed to come with living in the countryside. We valued the "everything-within-walking-distance" convenience that a moderate sized village offers. But what we seriously underestimated was the noise. The picture post card images of village windows with shutters wide open and lace curtains gently waving in the breeze do not come with a volume control button. There is a reason. Even French neighbors on the same street would wag their heads and complain of the noise made by the four or five "ruling families" that surrounded us. By sheer number of children, they dominated the street. And, although the Arab family across the street was not part of their social circle, they seemed to vie for airtime playing their music for the entire neighborhood: not the music of French romance: no Trenet, no Piaf, no Yves Montand not even a contemporary Diana Krall: nothing from the French cabaret genre, no French classics. The music of choice was a cross-cultural mix of Rap, Hip Hop, and contemporary selections from ghettos around the world with their characteristic bombastic base thumping through the walls with an occasional sprinkling of stale American music from the 1970s.

To cope, I would create my own imaginary interpretations of these invading sounds. After one of the children's parties, there appeared a new toy on the street. Within the first few moments, I could see that this was a gift given by some well-meaning adults who had no children of their own. It was a small florescent pink battery-operated automobile large enough for a two-or-three-year-old to ride atop. With a child aboard and watchful teen or parent behind it would grind along the street at an agonizingly slow speed. The decibels of the motor obscured the sounds of glee from its petit passenger. The offending cacophony, volume growing ever louder, approached. It bumped into doorsteps, then into the trashcans, 'til at last, it reached its destination in front of our house. A child's whine and the whirring sound of the mini motor called out for a parental *deus ex machina* to retrieve it, turn it around, and head it back in the other direction. The approach-and-return of this miniature Godzilla, continued for hours, batteries gradually wearing down, only to be recharged overnight. I was completely wrong in my estimates of batter-life, the child's level of interest and adult tolerance.

For the better part of two weeks Godzilla terrorized the streets with a tolerant teen appointed by parents to supervise the toddler, while the parents were safe and serene in their (silent) interior courtyard.

In time, we were able to name most of the children on the street, not because we had been introduced, but because we could hear so clearly as they called to each other, fought with each other, and on the rare occasion, were chastised when at last a parent arrived. For us there was no escape from incessant ambient noise. Closing the windows and shutters at the height of summer was not a possibility, although, in desperation we did try as the late-night chatter approached midnight, and when the amplified music from the bar around the corner became intolerable.

We learned the value of those prized inner courtyards as a place of refuge and peace. In them, the unpleasant sounds of village life are shut out, first by the outside walls, then by the airspace of the rooms inside, and then by the back walls of the home that faces onto the courtyard. This private cloister-like space gives those fortunate enough to have it a controlled environment – a private heaven which makes interaction with the noise of public life more bearable, taken in small doses. A village home with an interior courtyard is a prized possession. Most modest village houses have no courtyard and, if any, very limited outdoor space, hence there is a constant barrage of active street life in summer. It is common to have nightly gatherings of adults sitting on their windowsills talking, smoking, and having a cool drink to pass the time until midnight, when it becomes cool enough to sleep. *Cœur de Village* was just such a modest village house. Some outdoor space had been created in a roof top terrace, but it left us exposed to the noise of the street below.

September brought relief, not only from the summer heat, but from the constant noise. I write in our journal:

> It seems, since the school year has begun, and vacation ended there has been more quiet time. Thank heavens. This quiet is, of course, relative. We still had 15 children playing in front of our house after school, into the early evening. It was 4 pm when I first noticed the noise and 8pm when I could say "peace at last". Yes, I counted. It was a personal reality check. Was I being unreasonable? I tried to conjure up an image of tiny tots at happy playtime learning the basic social skills of sharing and group interaction. One might actually be charmed by the mental picture – and just think, how lovely, they even speak French! This image, and the related civil behaviors, lasts for about 10 minutes. These little darlings played - FOR

FOUR HOURS - like feral beasts, screaming their heads off at my front door. Yes, I counted them as they ran to and fro, in and out of the allèe, hopping up onto the garbage bins as they climbed the dividing wall like their own little Everest, bringing them eye to eye with my kitchen balcony, and as their football bounced off my front door used like a backstop. Yes, I counted. I was NOT being unreasonable this was awful. But, we were new to the neighborhood; new to France, and nothing in our classes at Alliance Française prepared us for this. .

Somewhere around 8pm they started to disappear, presumably to go home for dinner. With cooler September evenings, there is also some relief from the late-night adult chatter in the streets. Still, I have times when I realize that this rural village life is more intrusive, much noisier than our Chicago city life. In Chicago, this scene would have been remedied in a flash because we had the power of language and a sense of belonging. Here we are strangers

On the positive side, I have had some success on the "pooper patrol". That is, I've been able, with the help of jars and jars of *essence de moutarde* to eliminate the *crotte de chien* from in front of our house. I don't know whether to be glad or so, so sad that cleaning up after other people's dogs has become a part of my everyday life.

I feel I've retired to the public housing projects. Can you believe it, I identify "less noise" and "less dog shit" as a positive? Even the fact that the garbage dumpsters, across from our front door, are only mildly overflowing on Sunday evening reminds me of living in "The Projects". I try to be glad for these" improvements", but this was not my image of retirement to rural France.

Perhaps as we get settled there will be some possibilities to live life as I intended. But for now, I have accepted my routine of spraying mustard and an occasional sprinkle of cayenne pepper as normal. I take some measure of satisfaction in repelling dogs from the front of our doorstep. And I repeat this delightful task at the site of our future home at rue Molière. What a way to begin each day. But for the moment – success! This is a "poop-free" zone, until it rains!

Now if I could only find a repellent for inconsiderate children and their parents! (Just a joke?)

**Getting Settled**

We began settling into *Cœur de Village* in earnest. After all, this house was to serve two purposes; it was our own temporary residence and an eventual house to let. The interior of *Cœur de Village* was to reflect our same attention to detail, comfort and style as we had given to past renovation projects and it served as a practice pallet for the faux finishes and French wall finishes that would one day be used at le petit jardin de l'âme, the home we dreamed of at rue Molière. *Cœur de Village* was a simple village house, but we were able to make the most of every inch of its simple charm. As a result, it had character and class that made it stand out above its surroundings. During this time, we had a few early B&B requests and put them up in a spacious second bedroom with its own bath and private terrace. While we were pleased with what we had created inside and what we had to offer, there was a tension hanging overhead as to whether guests would be pleased with the neighborhood. I found myself literally sweeping and washing down the allée in front of our home and the street to either side, removing the offending crotte, tidying up the overflowing garbage bins - a permanent fixture, planted generally in disarray, about six feet from our door - and throwing a bucket of chlorine bleach behind them. At first, I would try to accomplish these tasks anonymously, but of necessity, I became more brave as time went by. It was nearly impossible to find a time when there was no one on the street. With each passer-bye there came some comment about how dirty it was, though never a thought as to a remedy. It seemed that my time spent on these tasks kept growing. Personally, the neighborhood behaviors were an embarrassment to me. I had never lived in a place of which I was embarrassed.
I write:

It is one of those rare cloudy days in the south of France, with a sprinkle of rain: the first such day since April or early May. I don't mind it. Our guests arrived last night after a long day of travel. Thankfully it was a quiet evening. I always "hold my breath" in hope that it will be quiet when we have guests, so embarrassed I am at the noise levels we live with from day to day. They have not really improved much. There is no substantial change, only the change created by the cooler weather, closed windows and shorter daylight hours. Having a few groups of guests now helps to provide a positive distraction and some working together for Linda and me. But we are clearly not in the same spot on the adjustments to this new life.

I looked forward to today. We worked so hard yesterday and have the lingering aches and pains. So today was to be a "Clean Day". I showered fresh in the morning rather than in the newly acquired (and necessary) habit of showering at the end of the day's grimy work. I was ready for a day that might approach what I would like someday to someday call normal. The antique faire in Béziers promised to be leisurely and interesting and we had some practical tasks to accomplish. I looked forward to today – and then today arrived!

During the night a garbage bag was haphazardly slung in the general direction of an already filled-to-overflowing dumpster. It sat precariously on the edge. When I first noticed it, it had not yet been pulled open by the band of dogs that frequently roam the streets in search of such treats. But I knew it was destined to be trouble as soon as I looked out the window. I knew the rain had washed away my *"Contra Chien, essence de moutarde"*, so I expected to have to renew the spraying. What I did not anticipate was that I would have to get up from the breakfast table, excusing myself from the pleasant conversation with our B&B guests. I heard more than one dog growling and pawing through the garbage. The choice: Ignore it, and have garbage strewn all around by (what turned out to be) 4 dogs pulling apart the sacks of garbage. -OR- Get up and clean up. There were already signs of the now all too familiar *crotte de chien* at my front door. I chose to act now. The dogs, of course, were reluctant to leave their breakfast recently plucked from the mangled sacks. But, I was not to be deterred. Taking an umbrella from inside the door, with a clever combination of maneuvers borrowed from both Zorro and Mary Poppins, I successfully shushed them away. A sight to behold! But more effective canine crisis management, I could not find. Then I swept up the garbage, cleaned up the poop, and sprayed *essence de moutarde*. What a nice start to the day!

After breakfast, I went to rue Molière. I knew that I would need to renew the mustard spray before rue Molière became a new doggie dumping ground. I was too late. Several dogs had deposited their rather large crotte de chien "calling cards". I picked it up, and sprayed. What a lovely way to begin the day – twice! Thus, the tone was set, and I began to "just get through the day". .

From about noon until five in the evening we had a moment of relief. The antiques faire, in Béziers was a pleasant distraction and we found a few treasures. I enjoyed being a tourist in France for the afternoon. .

We returned home to find the little savages in an imaginary battle in front of our house. Four boys age 8-10 years, whooping battle cries, ran up and down the street. I closed the window to diminish the volume. A nap was what I had in mind, but I was stirred from my bed when the shouting increased in volume and pitch. I got up to see what had happened. Three girls about the same age had joined them – or rather – were challenging the boys. They had raided the dumpsters and cardboard boxes to pull out Styrofoam packing materials from which they fashioned their imaginary shields and swords. Combined with sticks and bull rushes they taunted and shouted at each other until around 7:30 pm. At that point, the girls left, and the boys changed from combat mode to a form of demolition derby using their scooters. Remnants of the earlier medieval battle were used to form barricades and an obstacle course. Near 8 pm I could stand the noise no longer, so I escaped to the work site at rue Molière. I returned later in the evening in hope that all warring knights of the realm, distressing damsels, and stunt car driving wannabees had been called to their dinner tables. I picked up the garbage; swept the street of candy wrappers, broken Styrofoam, flattened soft drink cans, and other miscellaneous debris.

Such *joie de vie* is too much to contain.

It is silent for a short time, but it is like the aftermath of a hurricane.

And such was everyday life at *Cœur de Village*. Well, I exaggerate, not every day -- most days. On further consideration, the description above was the norm in front of our house. I briefly considered purchasing new property; perhaps adjacent to the school playground. There, at least, recess time is limited.

I would sometimes wander the village streets, in part as an escape from the noise, but also in search of a reality check. Were all streets in the village populated by terrorizing tots and pre-teens? Other streets, I found seemed free of children and less bombastic. To be sure, the blare of radios, CDs players and televisions is a common problem of village life, especially in warm weather. The young like it loud and the old cannot hear. But, I also noticed more quiet spaces. Perhaps the group of elderly women sitting daily on the corner of one street, kept their vigil for respectable silence; their mere presence every day claiming the space for more civil pursuits.

I also roamed the streets in search of an answer to another noise pollution question. Occasionally, I would be awakened around 1:00 am by the sound, no, make that the vibrations, of deep bass booming through the night air, and through my bedroom walls. Fortunately, I discovered that this did not emanate from the village bar closest to us. More unbelievably these deep vibrations came from the direction of a local "watering hole" down the street and around the corner. One night I went on a late-night reconnaissance mission. I sought to answer the question of just how many people were being entertained by this bombast? Perhaps I was a minority of one, who expected to sleep during the midnight hours. Getting out of bed, I dressed, and walked in the direction of these amplified palpitations. In the bar, under a Saturday-Night-Fever of lights and flashes, sat no more than six very sad looking people! I was flushed with feelings of anger and disbelief. But mostly, I just wanted to cry. The France of my dreams had become my nightmare.

Quiet periods at *Cœur de Village* were fleeting moments surrounded by long stretches of high volume. In addition to the almost daily sensory assault, I was becoming seriously sleep deprived. I wished to return to the civilized life I knew in our quiet, gentrified Chicago neighborhood. Our past life, while indeed more complicated, was more rewarding. Unfortunately, this new life in France was not less stressful.

When we received the third quarter financial statements on the status of our American investment portfolio, the horrible truth of the financial impact of September 11th came brutally to light. In round figures, we had lost one-third of the value of our portfolio. This was not as bad as some had projected, and we knew that we had time to re-build financially before drawing on this retirement fund, but it was clear that we could not afford to pick up and start over. Any thoughts of a major change seemed financially impossible to me. Fortunately, we had already set aside enough money to complete our projects both at *Cœur de Village* and le petit jardin de l'âme, but we realized that we no longer had a comfortable cushion. And worse, the feeling of being financially stuck set in.

None of this distress was reflected in our correspondence with friends. Only a very few knew of my general discontent. There was no intent to deceive those "back home". But there is a very strong image that France and Francophones have cultivated about France and the French life style. The romance of all things French is very strong. In part, I did not want to be the one to disillusion them, to rob them of their own French dreams: dreams of that trip to the French countryside, the images of lavender fields, endless rows of vineyards, fine wines, great cheese, gourmet foods and on and on. And for me, I hoped that this horror would pass and be forgotten.

## Halloween Approaches

I write to friends:

Dear Al and Ellie,

The French have imported the American version of Halloween. It is a rather recent import with some controversy. Most of the merchants look at it as an opportunity and many ordinary folks think it just ghastly (or is that ghostly). Traditionally the schools are on holiday for a week for All Saints / *Toussaints* -- of course, another reason for a vacation. But, many do not like the addition of the ghoulishness that comes with Halloween. Personally, I must agree with the conservatives on this one. (Oh, my God, I've become a conservative: when did that happen?) There's something foreboding about a cultural change that moves from celebrating All Saints to celebrating monsters. Of course, the children love the candy and the merchants love the cash. I say, give them a few years, and they will have to add security to avoid "devil's night" pranks that get out of hand. Well, enough of that sermon.

We have some news and progress on the construction: We had a bit of a slow down for a week or two with workmen not showing up, but we are now back on track. On one of her recent "walk-throughs" Linda found some mildew on the walls where the plaster has taken too long to dry. Then discovered mildew on boxes that were piled against wet plaster. We have been moving and sorting and rescuing books, linens, framed artwork, etchings and our clothes etc. Seems like we have avoided any serious damage. But, for a moment, we had this sinking feeling that we had successfully moved our art and furniture only to have it mildew in its packing boxes. Apparently, the plaster is so thick on the walls that it is taking a long time to dry. Our weather has been more humid and there is, yet, no central heat in the house where the plaster is being worked on. So now we have moved packing boxes (again) and placed portable heaters in the rooms for nighttime heat. It's one saga after another.

Back at *Cœur de Village*, we are finishing up the decoration of the living room on the ground floor. It's looking great now, but we had a lot of poor workmanship to re-do and touch-up to get it to look good. The exposed natural stone wall, it seems, will continue to be a problem with shedding. Perhaps the general mason was right on that one after all. But it is what we wanted, and it does look authentically rustic and original. Today, we were able to move down some of the furniture for the living room and Linda and one of the workmen will be putting in the plinth sometime this week. Then, we have pictures to hang when we are finished.

We hope that you will plan a return visit sometime to see the project completed - and not work so hard this next time. You are always most welcome.

Take care - Val and Linda

## Louis Quatorze

After having to cease all work at rue Molière for nearly nine months it was good to see progress at last. Every morning we "went to work", a commute of about five minutes' walk back and forth on the same village streets past the same village folk. We were so predictable in our comings and goings that the neighbors were able to give directions to deliverymen, workmen, and assorted passersby as to our whereabouts at any given time of the day. During this time, a pleasant relationship began with one of Florensac's Ambassadors of Good Will. Although we knew that this man had just celebrated his 90th birthday, we, in true French fashion, did not know his name. At 90 years of age, he was still alert, active and in "good form". I think of him as the Official Greeter in Florensac. A prisoner of war in Germany, he seemed partial to *les américains* and grateful still for America's role in the liberation of France in WWII. It was for me humbling, and gave me a sense of pride that he, like other old men in the village, remembered the USA so favorably, even while disagreeing with contemporary USA politics. Our conversations often started with the few English words he knew, "Good Morning", and concluded with, "Thank you", and "Bye-Bye". His Good Morning greetings had that lilting French melodic style of the *"Bon Jour"* which I had often associated with French. In time, Linda and I referred to him as Monsieur "Good-Morning".

One day as we were having our ritualized village conversation about the weather and what he was going to eat for lunch, he asked me my name.

*"Je m'appelle, Val."*

He looked puzzled.

I repeated *"Val... comme saint Valentin, comme février quatorze".*

He smiled and told me his name was *Louis*.

I said, *"... comme Louis quatorze !"* He got it! My first play on ords, a *mot d'esprit*, in French.

It was an honor but took some adjusting for Linda and me to call this venerable old man by his first name. Somehow linking him to one of France's great kings seemed fitting, for this was a grand old man. And, although I am sure that Louis is friend to many visitors and villagers alike, he seems a special friend to us, calling us his mes *enfants américains*. He has a special fondness for Linda who he sees every morning as she walks to the patisserie for morning bread and croissants. Louis has become an important and refreshing part of our new life in France.

## Not yet a petit jardin

At le petit jardin, our learning curve about the ways of workmen in the construction trades in France was like the slope of Sisyphus. An ever-evolving group of tradesmen and day laborers did much of the heaviest labor, but there was still plenty to do alongside them. It was a never-ending task to get the contracted *plombier, électricien, plâtrier, carreleur, ébéniste* to show up, let alone show up in the proper order. Long ago we had given up the expectation of perfection, but we were, by nature, persons of orderly habits. In our professional lives, it was necessary to be well prepared, to do our homework. We expected of ourselves a blend of basic competency and a willingness to learn from mistakes. The everyday uphill battle began with getting people to show up. Admittedly *we* were slow to learn, it was a constant surprise to us that people just did not show up. Not a few minutes late, often not even the same day. They just did not show up. Many times, there was not even the courtesy of a telephone call, no explanation.

Fortunately, we had discovered, quite by accident, a reliable worker, who spoke English, German, and French, who became our "right-hand-man". We became the general contractors. Things were looking up, but we were nine months behind, and winter was closing in. There was no heat, no plumbing, and we were still running the necessary electric supply point long distance from the garage to the part of the house that had been made functional for telephone, computer communications, and basic electricity for the workmen.

At last the time came to place the order for the garden tiles in our courtyard. In addition to the predictable required information such as size, style, and quantity, we went to the vender with a map and directions to our home to facilitate delivery. We selected a product resembling time-worn French stone to create a genuine Mediterranean feel to the courtyard garden. We checked and double checked the order form to make sure that it was noted that the narrow street at rue Molière necessitated a narrow truck for delivery, and that the map would be attached to the delivery form. The delay of several weeks for delivery was, by now, something to be expected.

Well, the tile arrived, or should I say nearly arrived. On the day for delivery we received a telephone call. Our stones were here. But they were nowhere in sight. From his mobile phone, the deliveryman told us that the truck could not bring the pallets of stone to rue Molière. The street was too narrow. They would be delivered to the public parking lot near the bus depot in front of the Mairie (City Hall). We could pick them up there!

In our planning, we knew that we would need to transfer the stone from our front door, (the anticipated delivery spot) through the house, and to a place near to the courtyard. We had not planned that the delivery of garden tiles was about to become a public event. More importantly, how were we going to transport these pallets of stone from the public parking lot to our front door? Summoning up all my conversational skills I began. I must tell you that the conversation that follows could not possibly reflect my stumbling French, searching for construction vocabulary which was, even in English, foreign to me. My irritation was eclipsed only by the irony that I, who have not an ounce of construction skill in my background, was having this conversation in the first place. The conversation went something like this:

> "The delivery charge included delivery to our front door, did it not?"

> "Yes, but the street is too narrow".

"Did you not use a (Oh, God! St Rita, and anyone who is listening, what's the word for "Forklift truck" in French?) *le chariot élévateur*, to load the stones to the truck?"

"Yes."

"Then, I propose that you use the forklift to bring the pallets from the parking lot to our front door."

"The forklift is at the warehouse."

"Then, go back to the warehouse, put the forklift on the truck, and return with your delivery."

Sensing my immanent defeat, I thought to myself, I cannot believe that I am paying them for this delivery.

At this point the telephone went dead. I assumed, a strategic disconnect. A few moments later, there was a return call and we began again. The pallets would be set off the truck in the parking lot, and we could do with them what we liked. End of conversation.

"Au revoir!"

And so, we spent five hours loading and unloading 15 wooden skids that contained the stone slabs and preformed steps. Fortunately, we had rented a 3½-ton truck for the day for another purpose. Therefore, we had some means of getting the stone from the parking lot to our doorstep. The deliveryman had used a hydraulic arm fitted to his truck to unload each pallet, never breaking a bead of sweat. He had deposited his delivery in a matter of minutes and was gone. Because each pallet was too heavy for us to lift onto our truck, we had to open each container, lift each stone from the pallet, and hoist it up to the truck. When the truck was filled, we reversed the process of unloading each stone and placed it in our "someday-it-will-be-a-dining-room", near the courtyard. There was some thought, but little time, to be really concerned for possible theft of the opened containers during our intermittent absences. Strangely enough, we were reassured of their security because we had attracted a small audience of on-lookers from the village. We had become the entertainment for the afternoon. Nearly 100-mètre carré (1100 square feet) of garden tiles each 5 centimeters (two inches) thick, some slabs were as large as 70 centimeters (28 inches) square, some 85 x 55 centimeters (33 x 22 inches). They were heavy. And we hugged each one of them. It took Linda, myself, and two workmen, five hours to do it.

After all that, it remained to lay each stone in the garden, that meant lifting each one again, and placing it in its final resting place. And some of it still needed to be carried up to the third floor for the terrace and pool. But that was for another day.

Remember, during this time, we were living in our temporary home, *Cœur de Village*, completing the decoration at that site, and simultaneously, supervising the gross construction work at *le petit jardin*. Back at *Cœur de Village* I wrote in our journal.

06 November 2001

> At last, a couple of nice days in a row, and I don't mean the weather! Two or maybe three – do I dare hope for tomorrow – where I have enjoyed the day minus the sound assaults. Oh, the children do still play out front, but the size of the group and the length of time for play is significantly reduced.
>
> Perhaps it has something to do with the cooler weather and the earlier nightfall. The noise is brief and more bearable. I also have taken to playing my CDs more freely to counter the outside noise. The garbage has been contained, and I spend most of my time indoors working on projects to finish the decoration. The combination of reduced noise, cold weather, and a cleaner neighborhood make for a more enjoyable environment.
>
> I am also pleased that we are nearing the end of our decorating at *Cœur de Village*. We will be putting the final

touches on the ground floor over the next few days. I enjoy working alongside you, my love. And I enjoy seeing this little house transformed. I find myself now hoping that our first renter will decide to delay his arrival. This of course would help us. It would be more pleasant to stay put in this house rather than move into more primitive quarters at *le petit jardin*. We are so far behind in our work at *le petit jardin*. His delay would also give us some time to enjoy this little gem. Personally, I am hoping that we can stay through Christmas. But, right now, I'll take two or three good days and hope for more cold weather – windows closed, reduced sound, and children playing inside their own homes – thank heavens.

As it happened, the person who had contacted us to rent *Cœur de Village* never materialized. We were not so disappointed because it meant that we could enjoy our little home for a while. We did not realize at the time that we would, in fact, be living in this temporary home for the coming two years.

01 December 2001

At last an evening of civility and comfort in our house at *Cœur de Village*. Just before our vacation to Rome and Malaga, and again this evening, we were able to enjoy our home. The last of the rooms is complete. In some ways it feels good to have an evening by the fire and a drink without the elements of renovation hanging in the air and scattered all around. I am glad it is completed, and it is a wonderful little space.

Our vacation trips to Rome and Malaga were refreshing and again we had a chance to remember what life is like for us apart from "lives under construction". For a moment I caught myself making the emotional connection of "it's nice to be going home" and realizing that "home" was Florensac and France. Briefly, it felt good, and I hoped that perhaps it was a sign of some inner adjustment and a sign that I would feel better about living here in the days ahead. I was wrong

Walking the streets and resuming our roles as general contractors soon brought back that depressing feeling. The renovation itself is progressing - slowly - but that is not the problem. It is the emotional and moral upheaval raised in the progress that trouble me. Each of our individual "ups" and "downs" and the questions raised about the integrity of the workers and the constant vigilance necessary to look out for our own best interest is exhausting and depressing.

I look around me and see that the space we created does what we intended. It nurtures the spirit and calms the soul, as we hoped. Yet as soon as this rises in me, it is taken away, sapped, drawn from me by the larger environment in which we live. Perhaps that is what makes the outside noise and incivility so abhorrent to me. They violate the tranquil space we have created in our home, in ourselves.

## The First Noël

In some ways, our first Christmas was exactly what we'd expected, a little difficult. We did not feel "home sick", but we were adrift without a real sense of the local customs, and yet, without established friendships to celebrate the holidays. It brought back memories of a long-ago period in our lives when we, once before, started our lives anew. And here we were again starting over. It was quiet, very quiet. It seemed to us in our first year that the French really did not celebrate Christmas. We did not expect the grandeur of Chicago's Magnificent Mile, a glitter with millions of tiny lights, but the lonely little red slipper hanging pathetically from the streetlight was so sad. The street decorations were beyond minimal. In their paucity they managed more to emphasize the darkness than shed Christmas light. And the shuttered windows looked foreboding in winter's night. In fact, Christmas was a very "low-key" event. It is celebrated behind closed doors and shuttered windows with family. Christmas seemed to hum along, a warm but quiet celebration extending through the holiday period into the Three Kings' arrival on January sixth. It seemed that St. Sylvestre, France's New Year's Eve, had more sparkle and pop than Christmas.

In time our Christmas would grow, and we would make a Christmas as we would make our home here, but this year, it seemed that Christmas was missing in action. We discovered that the local singing of Christmas Carols had no room for Christ this Christmas. There was a cute rendition of *Paddington Bear's Christmas*, but no scripture was allowed; an anomaly, since the concert was held in church. It was difficult to find a restaurant open for dinner reservations on Christmas Eve or Christmas Day. The Christmas Mass was in some other village at some other time. And, we discovered that a little snow for Christmas would have been much preferred to the drizzling rain.

**Christmas 2001**

Val J. Littman & Linda S. Korolewski le petit jardin de l'âme

Merry Christmas and a happy holiday season. We hope that our Christmas letter arrives for you sometime during these 12 days of Christmas.

This year was the year of the big move. You will hear no more of those anecdotes of anticipation of our move to France. We've done it. We are here. We arrived March 03. Since that day we have been adjusting … to the language, the people, the customs. Adjusting to "life under construction". We have lived out more "Year in Provence" stories than a book would hold. It has been a difficult year, but it is hard to get much sympathy when you tell people you retired at 53 and moved to the south of France!   In due time we expect to meet this change of life as we have met other big changes – so, stay tuned for the "…and they lived happily ever after" part.

Highlights from our year might just be chapters in a book:

- **The Zen of Picnics** (and no Martha Stewart) – The house we expected to live in when we arrived in March was nearly ready for us to inhabit…in July. We had picnic breakfasts, picnic lunches, and picnic dinners amid the construction – no kitchen, no stove.

• ***Pas de Monnaie, Pas de Problème*** (no money, no problem) The purchase of our PT Cruiser without money! Linda forgot the checkbook. The dealer told us to take the car, go home (45 km) and send him the check on Monday.

• **If These Walls Could Talk** The discovery of the ancient parts of our house under tons of old plaster. We have mud brick walls dating from the 12-16th centuries, a grand Roman Arch, an 18th century doorway and steps made of volcanic stone from around 1000 AD.

• **A New Work Ethic** Exactly how many holidays can you fit into the month of May? A comprehensive guide to why not too much gets done here during  N (fill in any month of your choice).

• **The *Fermeture Exceptionnelle*** A variety of explanations why a store/office/restaurant may be closed, despite the sign that clearly says it is open. Alternate chapter heading: Open Every Day Except When We Are Closed.

• **In Praise of *Essence de Moutarde*** One man's battle (mine) to keep from being buried alive in dog poop! It's everywhere. (Very effective dog repellant recipe available on request).

Our renovation will stretch well into the New Year. But, so far, the tales of our construction woes begin to sound like a perverse version of the ♪ Twelve Days of Christmas ♪.

| ….. 12 tons of plaster…♪…. 5 more months delay… Our 4th plumber plumbing…3 French friends…2 leaks above… And a bank account that dwindles everyday ♪ |
|---|

As you see, the creation of our dream gives us a day-to-day horizon that is often village-sized. We do not escape global events or terrors of our world, but this year we see the world from a different perspective. In our own small way, we see more and more clearly the need for a place where people can come to soothe their soul, refresh their spirit and reawaken their dreams – at   le petit jardin de l'âme.

Our New Year's plans this year continue our tradition of 20+ years but with a French touch. We retreat to a small hotel – this year a 17th century monastery-turned-hotel in Albi, France. We celebrate with a fine dinner and take time to set our personal and joint goals for the year(s) ahead.

Well, I've got to go. It's Saturday night and Monsieur "Marrons Chauds" across from the potagerie has some fresh roasted chestnuts for our evening snack by the fire. If I don't get there soon, they'll all be gone.

*Au revoir, a Bientôt, La paix toujours soit avec vous.*

# Dreams and Nightmares – 2002

*The balance of nature decrees that a super-abundance of dreams is paid for by a growing potential for NIGHTMARES.*
-Peter Ustinov

**The Everyday Face of France**

Our Christmas letter of 2001 was our public face for some distressing nine months of adjustments to life in France. The letter also reflected an attempt to keep looking at the bright side of things. A little humor and strong doses of irony helped me. Linda preferred to look for the silver lining somewhere in the darkness. But truly, we were alternating between despair and determination. The renovation was progressing, sometimes due to stoic perseverance. But, more often, I was despairing, and Linda was more determined.

The impact of these nine months raised several questions. Was our experience an experience of *la vie de France?* This was not the dream we envisioned. Were our experiences to be limited to this period of construction and renovation? Was this truly part of the process of acculturation to the ways of France, or was our experience with the renovation project the experience of a "sub-culture" of questionable practices within a segment of society with whom we would eventually have little contact in the future. Would this pass or be always with us in France? Whatever it was, this process was wearing on us individually and as a couple. In our individual attempts to cope, we were beginning to develop different world-views of this experience. We were drifting to opposite ends of the spectrum of interpretation. I saw something as black and suspicious, always hoping that I might be wrong. Linda saw it white, and rationalized her way through the darkness when it appeared.

For me, our unsatisfactory everyday interactions with workmen and tradesmen took on socio-cultural proportions. These men were, unfortunately, the face of France for us. These were the people with whom we spent most of the waking hours of our day-to-day life. This was France. Not the France of fine food and fine wine, not the France of celebrated craftsmanship, not the France of the witty repartee. In our little corner of the world, I did not expect to meet the next François Mansart, or André Le Nôtre, or a promising Colbert, Viollet-le-Duc or Pierre-Paul Riquet in apprenticeship, waiting to be discovered. But, this was, let's see: what's the French word for "banal"?

One day, I was working just inside the house with the doors open to the courtyard. Progress had been made with the plumbing, but we did not yet have running water, except for one tap in the garage. I heard a stream of water. Curious, I followed the sound. Had we sprung a leak somewhere? My discovery was a slight embarrassment to me, but our workman was a picture of nonchalance peeing into the water we used for mixing cement. That evening, at the end of the workday, Linda and I exchanged our stories, worthy of Ripley's believe-it-or not. It was then that I discovered that she had recently found it necessary to use chlorine bleach on a routine basis in the utility sink of the garage to rid it of the smell of urine.

We had become adjusted to the practice of "pee anywhere you wish", as an expression of French *liberté*. It was commonplace, even in this 21st century, to see men "marking their territory" along highways and country roads. The little passageway, which faced our home *Cœur de Village*, often smelled of urine. That they have very little thought to discretion bothers me not at all, at the roadside. But do these men have such small bladders, and even less control, that they must pee in my courtyard? Or, have we inadvertently hired workmen who failed basic toilet training? In any language what does one do? Hand out "Depends" on the first day of work? On another occasion, Linda appeared at the work site a little early following lunch one day. Her unexpected arrival seemed to have disturbed one of the workmen in a compromising position in the stairwell. From her report, she had clearly interrupted some private activity. We were never quite sure but "ejaculation interruptus" seemed best to describe his unzipped pants and the look on his face.

How soon could we remove this strange slice of humanity from our house? I certainly had not factored in dealing with miscellaneous body fluids as part of our renovation plans. Strange as it may seem, many months after the workmen had gone there were two spots in our garden in which I could get nothing to grow. A series of fully hardy plants placed in the soil of these two areas died inexplicably in a short time. When left in their pots, they survived. Eventually, "Eureka!" It dawned on me. These guys had been peeing in my planter boxes! We removed the dirt and started over.

I think further examples of this offending way of life are unnecessary.

In our never-ending search for suitable tradesmen of various skills we would, of course, ask for references. It was rare to find a satisfied customer among the French or English. One *carreleur* came highly recommended. His reputation was that he was good, but expensive. And we would have used him, but we were unwilling to wait eight months for him to begin the job. Based on our past experiences, we knew that "eight months" was his estimated start time and probably had little to do with the actual placement of tiles in our bathroom. The *électricien* was a recommendation from a French neighbor. We did use him. Technically, he was competent, and very charming. He was a bit electrifying himself, motoring up with his bright yellow Harley-Davidson between his legs. His *devis* for the work to be done was delivered in a glossy folder sporting the classic Marylyn Monroe publicity photo for *The Seven Year Itch*. This fellow had pizzazz. In fact, he, himself did very little of the work. It was left for "lesser lights" in his crew. There's more of the *électricien* story to come.

We searched for a *plâtrier*, twice. Our first man was excellent but landed in jail. Our second candidate gave us a good price. Which he adjusted upwards, twice, after he began. His first reason was that he had miscalculated the square meters of wall to be plastered; his second increase, he reasoned, was because the job was more difficult than he had expected and on his third approach, I showed him -in figures -that his latest proposed increase would have us paying him more than the going rate for plastering per square meter in the region. We were not looking for cheap labor: but he was the professional, he gave us the price for the job; he did not want to take advantage of us, did he? A few days later one of our other workmen came back from lunch with a tale that our *plâtrier* was telling the men at the local bar that *les américains* were no longer as generous as they used to be. Frankly, I hoped that everyone was listening!

Word had apparently not yet reached the neighboring town by the time we were looking for a *ferronnier*. In our search for a craftsman to create a handrail and some iron grillwork, we found a young man in the neighboring village. His estimate for the job was like the other candidate who came from a large city nearby. More importantly, he was the only artisan, so far, to give a written promise of delivery within a specific timeframe. I thought, "Here's our man!" We accepted the *devis* (estimate). However, when he came for final measurements we discovered a change. When we asked for a clarification, he informed us, "His wife had made a mistake". The mistake seemed to be in the calculation of the tax. The tax had been calculated at 19.6% (the usual Value Added Tax) rather than the reduced tax of 5.5% for renovation of old houses. His revised *devis* had the correct tax calculation, but the total cost remained the same. That is, we pay the same and he benefits from the difference in the tax! What? After listening to a creative accounting tale that would put even Enron Executives to shame, we sent him packing. We were not convinced that the tax benefit should end up in his pocket. We decided not to do business with him. After all, this was only day one! What further surprises were in store for us from this creative fellow?

We selected the more professional *ferronnier* from Béziers. He came when he said he was going to come, did what he said he was going to do, charged what he said he would charge. The job was done well and on time. Truly a miracle!

There followed a spurt of activity and renewed confidence. In March I sent an update to friends and colleagues

### Update from France – March

It's amazing! We are beginning to see the results of many

months (years) of work finally coming together. Oh, we are not finished yet, but the end is in sight. We have moved from the gross demolition and construction to the finishes at last.

We have electricity in most of the house at rue Molière. The electrician began his work in October, occasionally charmed us with his presence over the past five months, and is still not finished. He has recently taken to avoiding my telephone calls. In "counter intelligence moves" I have taken to making "stealth phone calls" from public phone booths so that he cannot recognize the phone number with his caller identification. Ah hah! I was successful in snaring him yesterday!

The tile-man arrived on time and has begun to set the tile for the master bathroom and our guest bath. We are very happy with the tile choices. The tile-man is very skilled and has managed to compensate for the loss (damage) of two boxes of tile during shipping. We had two extra floor tiles left over despite the breakage! Let's hope he can be as skillful in stretching the wall tiles, since we also discovered more breakage in those cartons.

And today, the plumber arrived to do some work before his vacation. He has recovered nicely from the initial snafu of a few (miscellaneous but necessary) pieces missing from the bathtub and the faucets that he ordered for us months ago. However, he has chiseled yet another channel into our "once-upon-a-time" pristine, newly plastered, primed, and painted bedroom walls. And now he's informed us that we will need to enlarge our chimney that, only recently, was successfully sealed against the rain. It seems that there is now not enough room to accommodate the various smaller chimney flues from the gas burning fireplaces (which of course he has known about for six months).

Our two regular general workmen were here today sanding what remains of our plaster walls on the *premier étage* (second floor) and doing general cleanup of tons of debris that will be taken to the dump on Monday. After the garbage is out, there will be room for the floor tile on the ground floor.

It was a real beehive of activity for today! At one point, it looked like a scene from "Keystone Cops". After months of delay and with over three thousand square feet of construction space, everyone converged today on the bathroom – one of the smallest rooms of the house!

Although progress was being made on the renovation, I was losing psychological ground and slipping into depression. Momentary successes were outweighed by the sheer emotional energy that it took to succeed. The search for the bright side and humor were no longer working against a daily diet of offensive behaviors, difficulties in communication, trickery, uncertainty, questions of competency, and sleep deprivation. I write in the journal.

16 March 2002

I searched out my fountain pen for this entry. It was a quest for some sense of civility, a miniscule remnant of a formerly genteel life. Yesterday, I had my first appointment with the psychiatrist in a nearby village. I agreed to go as part of our long-distance telephone counseling with a therapist we both knew from Chicago. Intellectually and professionally, I agree it is best to see if some medication will help. But there is an underlying sense of dread in taking this step. No, I am not afraid of the medication or of some stigma. In some ways I am afraid of "getting well". That is, I am afraid that once recovered from this depressive state the conclusion will be the same. That is, life in France as it has been experienced is intolerable. Depressed or not depressed the environment that "drives me crazy" remains unchanged. A new frame for a bad picture doesn't make it a good picture. But, I speak prematurely and hope for a different conclusion.

My experience at the clinic was in some ways a microcosm, once again, of why life in France is intolerable for me. I was able to overlook the shabby physical conditions. It looked like a former private home-turned-clinic, but with those poorly maintained rough edges of a public clinic; sterile, broken plastic chairs, no reception, and sadly in need of fresh paint. One poor plant struggling to survive without adequate light or care seemed symbolic in this minimalist décor, but these were superficialities. The doctor with whom I had an appointment came into the waiting room. It was clear; I was the only one who was not "a regular". I think, that despite my continuing interior decline, I must still look like a "squeaky-clean-American".

I began the conversation in French. I had prepared my opening lines to explain that I had a problem. I was an American living in France for about one year; I was seeking help for my depression and that I came for medication. I concluded by saying that I hoped he spoke English, since it would be easier for me to continue in English.

He responded simply, "No."

After a pause in which I was able to choke back my tears and frustration only partially, I said, in French, "Certainly you are making a little joke. I telephoned and asked for a psychiatrist who spoke English. And my appointment was made with you."

Again, he said, "No." No explanation, no apology. I thought that I had gotten myself used to this abrupt negative. It happens often in restaurants and commercial enterprises. But here, in the doctor's office?

The negative response to a client or customer's question is one word, "No". When we first arrived, we began many of our inquiries in France with the "five magic words" we learned as part of our preparations to come to France; *"Excusez-moi de vous déranger"* / Excuse me for disturbing you, followed by our question. But, too often, we were met with the monosyllabic response, "No". I have learned that the French do not apologize, and in fact, do not expect an apology. Even if the person responds with *"Je désole"*, instead of *"No";* the words, the tone and the shrug make *"Je désole"* sound more like "tough luck!" rather than "I'm sorry". There is nothing to convey an interest in helping; perhaps something like "No, but we do have this possibility", or "No, but perhaps we could help you this way." Just "No."

I continued in our journal:

> I remained in silence. Not only had I run out of script, I did not know what to do next, and I was afraid to open my mouth because the tears were so at the edge. Eventually, he said, in French, that perhaps the psychologist next door could help since she spoke some English. He got up from his desk and interrupted her (she was with a client). I could tell that he asked her to speak with me, and then he directed me back to the waiting room until she was available. He then left, not to go to his office: he left the building.
> As I sat waiting, there were many mental images passing through my mind. I had spent most of my professional life helping people to find proper services for their mental health, guiding people to professionals who were not only qualified, but who were a good match for the individual and their problem - a good emotional fit - thereby maximizing the potential for success; making it as easy as possible for them when they were in a most difficult and debilitating state. I knew the value of my services long ago, but I now found myself in exactly the situation that I had helped others avoid. Here I was, in a community mental health center, I did not know the local procedures, I had no knowledge of the credentials of the people to whom I was presenting myself. Adding insult to injury, I was not able to get the services I had come for. After about 30 minutes, the psychologist came into the waiting room. She was an older woman, seemed assured and experienced. She explained, that if I spoke slowly in English she would be able to help. She took a brief history that seemed to cover the basic assessment issues that I was so familiar with from

my own professional life. She then contacted the psychiatrist by telephone.

Within a few minutes I was escorted back across the hallway to the psychiatrist's office. He had returned. Before writing his prescription, he asked me a few routine questions; more to my amazement, they were in English!

I decided to pass over the confrontation that I wished to make. I just wanted him to write his magic formula, and I would be out of his office! My encounter with the psychiatrist was yet another disturbing disappointment. In some ways, because I expected more of a professional, it was another, but more disturbing experience of living in a culture where deception is a way of life. I did not expect to find here, in the psychiatrist, the same lack of personal integrity and mutual respect that I had come to experience from our construction workers. In my search for help, I encountered a repeat of the very experiences that brought me to this point.

P.S. As I write this journal entry, once again the music blares from the apartment across the street. Each time I ask them to reduce the volume, it is as if I've never asked before. Or, as has been lately, the occupants play a game of "hide & seek" avoiding being caught in the window, avoiding eye contact, so that my request cannot be made.

## A Monday Morning

It was a routine Monday morning about 10 am and this was the litany of life in France for the day, so far. Our faithful friend and worker, Gebbert, arrived on time as usual, but I could see it was a bad start to the week already. On the way to work Gebbert had stopped to pick up the day laborer who had begun on Friday. He was still in bed, and had decided not to work today. Gebbert knew us well enough to tell this unfortunate man that there was no need for him to think of working for us tomorrow either – or the next day.

*Et plus encore*, Gebbert was also searching for Guy, the tile-man, who had for some reason not shown up this morning. Guy has been doing an excellent job, but we were now in a time-crunch to get the tiles laid in the kitchen, so that the tile and glue could set up properly before the kitchen is installed early the next week

I telephoned the plumber who was to come last Thursday – but did not. He said he had troubles with his truck and could not come. I wondered if he knew that I have been rehearsing my French over the weekend to tell him how dissatisfied we were with the job he had done in our guest bathroom the last time he was here. A few sleepless nights, several consults with the dictionary and some advice from friends who had lived here a long time, and I felt prepared with both a script and a strategy to tell him he would need to do the work all over again.

After I convinced the plumber that we needed him to come to work tomorrow, I telephoned the vender who was to deliver our kitchen stove, the ventilation hood and back-splash. "Sorry", the receptionist said, "He has not in yet arrived". When will he arrive? She did not know. Will he arrive sometime today? She did not know. I settled for telephoning later in the day rather than leaving a message.

Then, to make this start to the week complete, I had to tell Gebbert that during yesterday's rain we found three leaks in our recently repaired roof. Two previous leaks had been repaired just fine, but they had spawned offspring, and we had a new family of drips in our *grenier*.

On a more picturesque note: As I walked to rue Molière this morning I saw, ahead of me, one of our neighbors and his four children pushing their two-wheeled wooden wagon down the narrow street. It was spring holiday, and I knew from seeing this scene before, that they were off to the field somewhere to collect *"souche"* / old dead vines for firewood. They, like many families in the village still used wood stoves as their primary source of heat. Although spring had arrived, the nights were still cool and damp. Coming toward me was a scene right out of Victor Hugo's, *Les Misérables*, Monsieur, and his children going to the fields in search of firewood. Later in the morning, they returned with their wagon filled to overflowing, papa pulling and the others helping to hold the precariously balanced load in place. I am sure that the children were ready for a warm lunch and a long nap.

## The Kitchen Arrives

Yes, I remember it well.

Well, let's see where to begin? Today is the long-awaited day of the arrival of the kitchen.

Keep in mind that this is the day of the grand metamorphosis! We have brought this room in our house from a room built sometime between the 12th and 16th centuries into the 21st century. Our "some-day-it-will-be a kitchen" was probably, at one time a stable. It had a dirt floor, stone sink, rustic beams no plumbing, no electricity, but lots of charm. Over time we have created a floor, cleaned the beams, removed the stone sink to our garden, re-created a window where there once was a window and put the door back to where we think it was years ago. We have brought the wonders of modern electricity and plumbing into this space. Today it all comes together, we hope. God willing. And we need a few miracles with the French workmen.

Guy, our tile-man, who had worked last week in the middle of the night to meet today's deadline has laid the floor tile with enough time for it to dry thoroughly. The plumber has, so far, ignored our attempts to complete the rough plumbing before the cabinetry goes in. Even my basic ignorance of these matters tells me this is a problem.

The kitchen furniture is due to arrive today. Our "kitchen people" have been wonderful. They have made by hand the kitchen furniture to our specifications. They are among the very short list of workmen so far, who have produced their work on time. We delayed them two weeks ago because other pieces of the puzzle were behind schedule. We have managed, cajoled, pleaded, insisted and now we have a confirmation that our kitchen stove, ventilation hood and backsplash will also arrive this morning between 9 and

10 am. I'll spare you the agony of our various attempts at setting a delivery date. It was like playing "pin the tail on the donkey".

The kitchen people have, of course, arrived on time. This is a picture of professionalism and order that I now only dimly remember from my former life. Within 15 minutes, they have a question about the plumbing. (Told ya!). Ten o'clock arrives and I have secretly regressed to saying Novenas to Saint Anthony, St. Jude and St Rita (respectively, patrons of the lost, the hopeless, and, my self-appointed patron of all French workmen, St. Rita, the impossible). "Please, please let the kitchen stove, etc., show up sometime today". From lessons learned in the past year in France, I decide to telephone once again and see if I can get yet another confirmation that the delivery will happen today. Our friend Gebbert intervenes and discovers that the delivery truck is in Florensac, but cannot find our street and is about to make the two-hour return trip to the depot. (Forget the fact that there are maps of the village posted in strategic locations in town like most villages in France). Gebbert runs out to capture the deliveryman. All three pieces arrive, and are the correct three pieces (minor miracle). The deliveryman leaves them in the street in front of our door and takes off like lightning. Although this delivery was free, it seems not to have included placing the stove in the proximity of the kitchen.

By now various neighbors have arrived to inspect the packages. At their advanced ages, none of them can help lift the stove, hood, and backsplash from the street into the house. Eventually, it happens (miracle number two). We have an odd but effective assortment of helpers. Gebbert, tile-man Guy, the kitchen people, and our Muslim medical student/day laborer make it happen with a musical mixture of French, English, German and Islamic grunts and groans.

And now, if only the plumber would arrive or return our phone calls.

Since the noon hour is approaching, I now expect nothing. I have learned that there is a finely-honed skill developed by all tradesmen early in apprenticeship; do nothing after eleven o'clock that has even the remotest possibility of interfering with an on-time arrival at the table for lunch.

After lunch, Gebbert informs me that the plumber had just returned one of our calls and indicated that we should go ahead and install the kitchen furniture, countertop and appliances, and he will move them out again when he comes, next week, to work on the sink, dishwasher and stove! I overlook the incredible, and find a way to say that the cabinetry and counter top are not movable. They are fixed permanently. Keep in mind, this is me, who knows next to nothing about installing a kitchen, telling the plumber that the kitchen cabinets and counter tops are not easily set-aside for him when he decides to appear to do his plumbing. (What planet have I been abducted to?) At last, he agrees to come – *toute suite*.

He arrives, and it is immediately clear that he will be staying the rest of the day. I thank him for coming, he replies *"Bien sur / Certainly"*, as if it were the most natural thing in the world for him to be here. At last, all the key characters and materials are in the same room on the same day. It's 3 pm.

It was a joy to behold the success of assembling all the necessary workmen in one place, albeit a little late in the day. But such a moment was to quickly unravel, as those who arrived first, were ready to end their day. I believed the kitchen people when they said they would return tomorrow they had a history of being true to their word. But, I would be a fool to let the plumber out of my sight. I indicated that Linda and I would be working in the house late that evening; therefore, he could stay as late as he needed to finish the job. I felt, with some satisfaction, that I had communicated my expectations successfully when he worked until past seven that evening. And he returned the following morning!

Eventually, we were able to take the necessary steps to use the kitchen, but at this time, we put it all under several layers of plastic to protect it from the remaining construction dust and the carelessness of the workmen. It was lovely, and, we were very pleased with our choices and amazed that it was all installed. Tomorrow there would be a lot of construction cleaning-up to do, then beams to dust, polyurethane to apply, and walls to prime and paint. Perhaps then, we would begin to unpack our kitchenware, which we last saw in Chicago, February 2001.

The effect of a couple of successful negotiations, and the sight of a kitchen that looked like a kitchen put some "wind back in our sails" and gave us a badly needed shot of self-confidence. We could sense the approaching finish line. We were also experimenting with a change in our management style. It was time, perhaps past time, to turn from the cautious, collaborative, conciliatory style of our first year. Collaboration only works when you are working with collaborators. Sometimes, a more Napoleonic style of management is in order.

**Up-date from France – May**

> *Les chantiers avancent. Tout le monde travaille aujourd'hui.*
> The construction advances. Everyone is working today

> Today, we have workmen scurrying about like ants at a picnic. Perhaps, because of the Spring break followed by the holiday yesterday, they have found a burst of energy! May is notorious for the number of holidays, except, of course, for the months of July and August in which virtually nothing gets done. French Labor Day, *Fin de la Guerre*, Ascension Day, Pentecost, and Mother's Day, all fall in this merry month of May. These holidays are combined with the occasional "*jour du pont* / bridge day" to connect the holidays to the weekends which precede or follow them. This narrows down the workweek to a precious few days.

> We are fortunate to have the work progressing. Our neighbors remain pleasant to us but are beginning to express their displeasure with the various workmen. There was a "Kodak moment" at 8:30 this morning as "Madame Blonde" in her night dress, shouted from her balcony to the workers…" too much dust…. too much noise": She called the local police who came to placate both parties. A little touch of hysteria to spice up the morning, and then, everyone shrugged their shoulders and went on as if

nothing has happened. Personally, I think that tempers seem to be a little hotter because our most visible workers on the façade of the house are Arabs. The political climate during this month of elections has heated up over France's immigrant population. Our permit from the Mairie allows us to block the street temporarily, but it doesn't do much to reduce frustrations. No one could be looking forward to the end of the renovation as much as we are.

There are a couple of signs that our acculturation to the ways of the south is progressing. The first, I call "**Battered by Builders Syndrome**". At the mere sight of a workman at our doorstep we get light-headed, our pulse quickens, and we enter a near swoon. We instantly forget the past months of neglect and the inevitable future of abuse. We shower him with gratitude – his eminence has arrived! The second sign is that we have better learned to stand up to these same delinquent dilatants.

In these recent days, Linda and I have begun to refer to the work site at rue Molière as the "war zone". In part, because no one room is yet complete. It looks like a bomb has exploded with stone, cement, plaster and plumbing materials used as shrapnel. However, our reference is mostly to the verbal and emotional battle zone that each day seems to bring as we try to hold these various workmen to completing their tasks.

We are still fledglings with our French. But no French Class could prepare us for these situations:

Two workmen and ourselves standing in front of the guest bathroom door trying to figure out how to get both handles on the double doors to operate properly. The door was specially made because the size was unusual. They were made as double French doors, to open simultaneously, as you put one hand on one door handle and one hand on the other door handle. The carpenter has installed them so that one door opens by pushing the handle down and the other by pushing the handle up.

Currently, in order to open the bathroom doors, our guests will need to pretend that they are driving on the Dan Ryan Expressway and wish to make a sharp right turn. They must pull one handle down with the right hand, and push the other handle up with their left to open this door (no turn signals necessary). Admittedly, the mechanism is a little tricky. By now we have learned one more way of responding when workmen say, "It can't be done". We say, "It doesn't have to be done today. Think about it for a few days. I believe that you will come back with a solution. We've heard that nothing is impossible in France". As we struggle in French, this comes out something like : *"Il ne doit pas être fait aujourd'hui. Pensez cela pendant quelques jours. Je crois que vous reviendrez avec une solution. Nous avons entendu que tout est possible en France, n'est-ce pas ?"*.

The man who repaired our roof has, at last, we think, corrected the leaks that sprung up after his first repair. To solve what seemed a mystery, Linda crawled up on to the roof herself to analyze the situation with the workmen and pointed out what needed to be done. Surprise, no more leaks. The same workman's replacement of the old ceramic tile gutters at the front of the house was an equally poor job. The excuse given for the poor job was that the old tiles were poor quality. This workman seemed to forget that we bought the antique tiles from him. So, we withheld his pay for that part of the job. To repair the work, the old tiles will be removed again. Some will break in the process. We have already purchased replacement tiles from a scavenger of architectural artifacts, and have asked the mason who is working on the façade to do the tile gutters once again. At these prices, the gutters should not only collect the rainwater, but also bottle it for sale.

And the plumber would like to be paid more on the account. No problem – except that the amount he wants to be paid would pay him nearly in full for a job not yet completed. Although much work has been done, none of the sinks, toilets, water heater, dishwasher, stove or gas fireplaces are working yet. After a sleepless night for Linda, and a breakfast strategy meeting of our own, we have come up with a plan. We will pay him half of the amount he is expecting, which will bring our payments up to 75% of the job. The remainder will be paid when all things are working. Since our French is limited, we will explain this using numbers. We drew up a chart to identify the payments made and the percentages to date. We added the phrase - *Le restant, 100%, quand tout est en état de fonctionnement* / The rest, 100%, when all is functioning. Linda meets with the plumber this afternoon. I am seeing my therapist!

Under the layers of stucco and cement on the front of the house we have discovered some handsome stones and will be able to finish the façade in a style called *"pierre apparent* / stone apparent" to highlight the large stones as much as possible. Our stonemason is confident that he can camouflage those areas where there has been some "re-muddling" over the years by renovators of questionable taste. We visited the local "stone tailor" recently. He has carved new window ledges from stone to complement the stone frame around the front door and to replace a few strategic stones that have disintegrated over the years. The façade will be simple, but interesting, and will show some of the changes over the centuries: where an arch was replaced, where a window was re-sized, and where the roof was raised. We have made our own mark in antiquity by adding a decorative oval window – an *"œil de bœuf"*- and the window ledges.

Gebbert is quietly working on the mud brick walls (from the 12$^{th}$ - 16$^{th}$ century) that we are preserving in one of the guest rooms. He comes to our aid often as a translator and adviser. It is sometimes difficult to keep from putting him in the middle of the verbal battle zones.

We are trying to get as much work as possible out of Adib -- our medical student/day laborer -- before he returns to classes in September. He is a clean and precise worker, and right now, he is our little spot of calm at le petit jardin de l'âme.

Lunchtime has arrived. The stonemasons are setting up their Bunsen burner to grill sausages in our "someday-it-will-be-a living room" and others are off to get some bread at the boulangerie. We leave for our own lunch and to brace ourselves for the afternoon. We are excited and optimistic – but very tired.

**La Saison Commence**

*"La saison commence. L'été arrive* / The season has begun. Summer is here!"

This is a phrase we hear from the restaurateurs, shopkeepers, and village folk. It announces the gradual change of spring to summer here in the south of France. The sun is still spring-warm, but some days, we get a preview of the summer-hot sun to come. This is the time of the year that we begin to seek out the shady, cooler side of the street in the afternoons, rather than the sunny side, when going to market or doing errands. This is the time of the year when we begin to think about "making reservations" at our favorite restaurants rather than just dropping in. Boats, traffic, and the number of children increase, as well as, the number of languages heard. Tourists have been increasing since the school holiday in April, but it is at that time of year that we begin to cross the threshold from seeing the occasional traveler, to adjusting our lives to the influx of summer tourists. A couple weeks ago we became tourists ourselves for a day. We packed up our beach chairs and parasols and a good book, for a quiet morning of sun, sea, and the Mediterranean breeze.

After little more than a year, I still feel very much like a foreigner. But, to some, we must look like we belong. Last week some French-speaking tourist stopped me in the village street to ask directions to Montpellier. Even more surprising, I was able to tell him with confidence how to get back to the *autoroute* and in the direction of Montpellier. Another asked where the *distributeur automatic billetterie* /ATM or Cash Station was located. Linda now has many familiar *"Bonjours"* and small conversations with the little old men she meets during regular evening walks along the levy around the village. And many people – the hairdresser, the butcher, the owner of the Tabac, and, of course, our neighbors – ask how the work is progressing on the house. Even my "shrink" asks – perhaps for therapy related reasons – about the progress of the renovation and our most recent confrontations with the workmen. I don't know if he is just curious, inquiring about my well-being or really does think I am crazy for building a pool on the *2eme étage* / third floor.

One of the more challenging moments this month was the purchase and delivery of three cubic meters of stone to be used to build the dry-stone wall for the raised flowerbed in the garden. Against our better judgment, we purchased this stone from a vender we do not like, but who seemed to be the only one who had what we wanted. We arranged for the delivery date, and I clearly advised them that the street at rue Molière was a narrow street, so that they would plan accordingly to deliver the stone to our front door. The sales person assured me "*pas problème* / no problem".

The day of the delivery came. Morning turned to late Friday afternoon. I had a feeling of *déjà vue* from the delivery of our garden tiles six months previous. I got concerned. My telephone call revealed an all too familiar story. The delivery truck was too wide to bring the stone into the street. They proposed to unload the stone at the post office, and we could carry them stone by stone to our front door. I did not know whether to be infuriated that this was happening again, or to be grateful that I already had a script in French for this situation. I'd been here before, different vender, same attitude. But I was ready!

I responded, that I paid for delivery of the stone to my front door not to the post office. Mental images of my past professional life -- my many hassles as EAP Director with Managed Care and Insurance companies -- flash before me. They helped me feel rather confident this time. Over the telephone I began the step-by-step three-way conversation with the deliveryman, the customer services person and myself. I reminded them that they have a hand operated hydraulic lift in their parking lot that is used to deliver heavy objects to small trucks and autos. I suggested that the deliveryman return to the main store load the hydraulic lift onto the truck next to the pallets of stone. Then, when he arrives in Florensac, unload the hydraulic, place the pallets of stone on the hydraulic, and push them to my front door much as he would push them across the store's parking lot. *"Voila!"*

This time it worked! Now I know why my hands have so few construction calluses and bruises, but it is my head that hurts at night. By now it is nearing 5pm. Gebbert and Adib stay behind to help us once the stone arrives. Linda, Gebbert, Adib and I form a hand-to-hand relay to get the stones from the front door of the house and into our living room before evening comes and the weekend begins.

Gebbert says that we will be able to move into *le petit jardin* during the summer – I hope he is right. Mustapha, the artisan for the façade, has finished the front of the house. It looks great! Unfortunately, Bernard, the *tailleur de pierre*, broke the new stone steps as he was wrestling to put them in place at our front door. He assures us that he will repair them, and it will never be noticed. We assured him that his estimate and bill for the work was for new cut stone steps, not repaired broken steps. We have yet to see where this part of the story ends.

Our plumber has been much more docile since Linda met with him last month. It seems he better understands us when we speak in Francs rather than French! He will be paid the remaining 25% when the job is finished, when the hot water runs and all the toilets flush. He does not smile as much, but the work is getting done. And Guy seems to have found the solution to finishing the fountain and decoration above the water line of the pool. This is plan "C", and I hope it works this time. Completion of the gross construction/renovation begins to take on some sense of urgency. We realize that we have about 3 or 4 more weeks to push the workmen to the finish line before the summer doldrums set in and the July/August *"vacances"* begin.

Last Friday evening, Linda and I sat in our garden at *le petit jardin* with a glass of wine. We were stealing a moment to anticipate what it will soon be like. After the other workmen left for the weekend, we stayed behind to wait for the electrician to return and reconnect our telephone, which had somehow, accidentally, been disconnected during the work earlier in the day. Our "garden" is not yet much of a garden, but we are beginning to see what the finished product will look and feel like. We are pleased. The garden tile is laid and looks wonderful. The neighbors' walls and glass block windows have been successfully – and tastefully – camouflaged to everyone's satisfaction. We have, at last, found a home for the old stone sink. And, the barbecue of *Pierre de Ardèche* is handsome in its place – but not quite ready to be used. I planted a few geraniums in one of the planter boxes that I think is out of harm's way from the hazards of future construction. Still to be done: the gutters need to be finished; the water cistern under the garden floor needs to be cleaned and made watertight; and the stones, which are resting in our living room, need to be made into a wall for a raised flowerbed. We are sad that our *Hibou* / White Owls have relocated to a neighborhood less crowded with scaffolding, jackhammers and construction workers. I guess relocating was the wise thing to do. The *Hirondelles* / Swallows still swoop in like a "Blue Angels" precision flying team, and the *Tourterelles* / Turtle Doves can be heard in the quiet. Some days my dream of genteel country life seems still far away. But we are more seasoned and one more season closer to le petit jardin de l'âme.

> *Will the future ever arrive? ...*
> *Should we continue to look upwards?*
> *Is the light we can see in the sky*
> *one of those which will presently*
> *be extinguished?*
> *The ideal is terrifying to behold,*
> *lost as it is in the depths,*
> *small, isolated, a pin-point,*
> *brilliant*
> *but threatened on all sides*
> *by the dark forces*
> *that surround it,*
> *nevertheless, no more in danger*
> *than a star*
> *in the jaws of the clouds*
> -Victor Hugo, *Les Misérables*

## Feux d'Artifice, François d'Assise and Folies Française

Well, it's only July 02, but fireworks are already flying here at *le petit jardin*. Summer's sun, notorious "French Resistance" and "Project Gridlock" in several areas have combined in an explosive mixture.

Guy has completed the work around the pool and fountain -- or rather, he has told us he is finished. He has told us three times that he is finished. We have in turn pointed out to him areas that, in deed, are not yet finished. He looks surprised and goes back to work on the project. Gebbert initially recommended Guy, but now has changed his tune, and we have a "family feud" among the construction workers. Beside differences of opinion on how the work should be done, it seems that Gebbert purchased, for his personal use, a lemon of a truck based on Guy's recommendation, and now, cannot get his money back. Also, it is reported that Guy often leaves the worksite with more tools in his truck than he came with. Surprise, surprise, Gebbert seems to be missing some tools.

Gebbert, in an effort worthy of Francis of Assisi, has now become the owner of a Pit Bull. It seems that the new proprietor of the local bar discovered that his patrons were a little squeamish of the Pit Bull's presence on the welcome mat at the bar and was looking for a new home for his Pit Bull. Gebbert, who already has three dogs and seven goats, a tiny aging caravan for a home and a lemon for transportation, took the Pit Bull, so that it is not given to someone who would train the dog for combative dogfights. Gebbert shows up in our courtyard after lunch with his new pet, "Diva".

We did not realize that we had a problem until the next morning, when Diva arrived with Gebbert, accompanied by a water bowl, food dish and blanket. Not long afterward, Linda received the first territorial growl and bark from Diva. Coming from a Pit Bull, this is an aria to send chills up your spine. During lunch we had one of our strategy meetings. The Pit Bull must go. The second growl later in the day confirmed it. We told Gebbert that since he already knew that we did not allow his other dogs in the house or the dogs of other workmen, we expected that the same limits would extend to Diva. It seems that we inadvertently placed the proverbial straw on the camel's back. Gebbert let loose with a litany of problems: his health, his car, his insurance or lack of it, his finances, etc. At this moment Gebbert's solution to this is to quit. It seems we have our own little Employee Assistance Managers Training scenario right before my eyes. After meeting this afternoon, I believe we are back on track, and we did not have to use our "Management Plan B". Gebbert is committed to finishing the project. And Diva will not be camping out at *le petit jardin* after all.

We believe (again) that we have successfully repaired the roof leaks. But of course, we will not really get to test this out because there is not likely to be a drop of rain here again until October / November. And with a similar irony, we will be testing the heating system sometime in July / August, after the plumber finishes his work.

Our derelict plumber has had some time to develop his RSVP to our proposal in May. He tells us that he will finish our plumbing project "when he gets around to it". Or, he proposes that we increase our payment to him (an amount slightly less than he originally asked for in May). We return the volley, saying that we will cheerfully increase our payment to the account on the day he shows up to finish the job. He is coming tomorrow.

Some days we seem so close to finishing, and yet, only yesterday we hauled another dump truck load of construction garbage out of our living room. I look forward to a day when cleaning the living room does not mean loading up a dump truck. Speaking of cleaning, Linda took on the job of preparing the large stone roman arch for its reparation by the *tailleur de pierre*. This arch is a striking architectural feature. It spans the full width of the living room and separates the living room from the dining room. This meant wire brushing and cleaning off creosote from the arch. The old stone shows through nicely. The effect on the arch is wonderful. The effect on Linda, turned her into a coal miner for a couple days. But she sure does scrub up nicely after a soak in a tub!

On occasion we are finding some time for fun. Recently, all of Europe was cheering for their favorite in the World Cup Football/Soccer. Then, there were a few surprises served up at

Wimbledon. Tonight, the big buzz in town is *Toro-Piscine* near the edge of town at the Boules Court. Posters went up around town yesterday, and today a truck with a loudspeaker played "matador music" while driving around town. I don't really know what to expect, but from the hype, it sounds like *Toro-Piscine* is to rural France what "Cow Chip Bingo" is to small town USA.

It turns out that *Toro-Piscine* is a parody of the Corrida, a bullfight *à la française*, or more accurately a *Corrida Camarguaise*. A *Corrida Camarguaise* is not a fight at all. It is more bravado than brutish, requires more Gaul than glamour, and more defiance than dual-to-the-death. It is an "I-dare-you-dance "between the young bull (the four-legged variety) and young "bulls" of the two-legged variety. The young men are more like contestants in a game show than Matadors. The contestants taunt the bull and try to get as close as possible, to pluck a flower or ribbon from the bull's horns. They dash away, usually with the bull in close pursuit. The *Toro-Piscine* parody places a very young bull in a shallow pool of water (the piscine). Last night's "star" was wearing green florescent tennis balls on the tips of his horns. Various games are played which require the young men to get as close to the bull as possible, scoop up a bucket of water from the bull's pool, and dash back to fill a container with water. Presumably, the individual or team with the most water in their container, and no tennis balls stuck in their derriere, wins a prize that makes all this worthwhile. Is this a world-class sports event or what? Should *Toro-Piscine* ever become an Olympic sports classic, remember you heard it from Florensac first.

The night breeze is pleasantly cool. It is good sleeping weather; not that either of us have any trouble falling to sleep. Our days are often both physically and emotionally exhausting. However, getting a good night's sleep remains a challenge. Some nights we are adults with a child inside. Our construction and acculturation anxieties seem to loom larger in the night. We turn to each other. Simultaneously, we give voice to our child's memory of journeys long ago. We sigh, "Are we there yet?"

### An Update from France – August

> It rained today. For us, in August, this is a rarity. Better still it is a gentle rain; no one rushing for cover, no thunder or

lightning, just a gentle sprinkle of crystal-like drops dancing in rivulets running through narrow streets. This is my chance for some rainy-day reflections on this summer's progress.

My expectations for advances in construction during this big vacation month had been adjusted to near zero. Therefore, I am happy to say we have accomplished a lot. The pool and terrace are at last completed and we have been able to use them. This will be a private place for us on our third floor / *2eme étage* with a view of tile roofs and the distant mountains. The *ébéniste* / wood worker surprised us with the completion of our wooden shutters for the front of the house and the grillage for the top of our terrace. We planted a small olive tree in a *Vase d'Anduze* and will be searching for other plants soon. Gebbert finished the stone garden wall on the ground level. Linda hauled nearly a ton of *terre vegitale* / garden dirt in the PT Cruiser – in several small trips -- to fill these raised flowerbeds. We found our garden fountain. I have planted plants. And, at last, we have a garden at le petit jardin de l'âme.

We have had our share of B&B guests during this month, as well as a visit from dear Chicago friends. With them we celebrated the first meal prepared on our kitchen stove and served it in the garden! We ignored the remnants of construction around us and concentrated on good friends, good food and the work so far accomplished

We still live in the small house at rue *Cœur de Village* but hope to begin the move to *le petit jardin* sometime in October / November.

The kitchen balcony at *Cœur de Village* provides us with memorable scenes and sounds of village life. The *allée* in front of our house at *Cœur de Village* is a favorite pedestrian walk to and from the market place. Recently, three young children were returning from their morning errand. They must have been sent to the *boulangerie* for the breakfast breads. On their return through the *allée* their imaginations cast a spell. With the chant of a giggle and the wave of their hands, their baguettes became swords and light sabers in a skirmish that must be hundreds of years old. Magically, battle implements became baguettes once again as they reached the end of the *allée*. They bit into the crusty end of the bread that seems irresistible to young and old alike here in France.

My own imagination was stirred by the site of the traveling fruit and vegetable vender. Two farmers in a battered Citroen truck announced the sale of peaches, melons, onions, and potatoes from the back of their truck. A rustic animal horn was used to trumpet their arrival. The simple, haunting sound reminded me of Anthony Quinn as Zampano in the Federico Fellini film *La Strada*. I waited for the truck to approach and called out from the balcony. "*Je voudrais quelques pêches. Combien?* / I would like some peaches. How much? "I went down to the street and bought a crate of white peaches for three euros: much more than we could eat, but, so delicious.

There is still much to do. Currently Gebbert and Adib are working on the vaulted ceiling in the passageway from the garage to the garden. We are so fortunate to know someone who sees our fantasies as creative challenges rather than impossibilities. With his help we will be able to change a nondescript passageway into an interesting and attractive space to delight the eye every time we walk through it. The cistern, under the garden floor, still needs significant repairs. We still need handrails on the stairs and tile on the living room and dining room floors. And, we still have one evasive plumbing leak that has kept us from moving in and using our master bedroom and bath. Linda and Gebbert believe they have found the source of the plumbing leak, but the strategy for attacking the problem is not certain. It seems that we may have to go at it from below, through the old wooden beamed dining room ceiling. This seems preferable to approaching it from on top, which would involve removing the tile floor and two layers of concrete. Our plumber is, of course, on vacation.

For the most part, we are now into the more detailed work of patching nicks and bumps in walls in preparation for primer coats of paint. Although there is a fine coat of dust over everything, we can see that soon this will be home! Of course, after the construction work is finished our decorative work begins. We have always found this to be more a joy than a chore. I look forward to a time when the cement mixer in our dining room will be replaced with a real dining room table and the antique chandelier that Linda gave me as a gift four years ago. Soon, the way of life we hoped for will have a space to grow at le petit jardin de l'âme.

The last plumbing leak proved to be relatively simple fix. And, as it turned out, was not the plumber's fault. But, it was a disgusting surprise.

The real story behind this leak begins in the years before our move to France, and long before the opening pages of this book. It had been lying there hidden under the concrete floor of the bathroom, and above the old planks of the dining room ceiling, just waiting until we thought we were finished. It would not be discovered until water was supplied to the toilets and they were in use on a regular basis.

In the years prior to our move to France we would make "working-vacations" of our visits to France. We would meet with masons who had been chosen by our building manager at the time. We would discuss and contract for specific projects essential to the structural integrity of the house and basic items such as the placement of the evacuation mains drainage system. These things could and should be done long before the finer elements of basic plumbing and electricity. During one of our visits we noticed that the main drainage from our master bathroom had been placed in the wrong spot. The plan had been made and measurements drawn, but in the end, the drain for the toilet in our master bathroom and the adjacent guest bathroom were about two feet from their intended spot. The building manager first suggested that we work around this error. After some consideration, we discovered that working around the error would mean that our master bathroom would be considerably smaller than we wished, and the guest bathroom considerably larger than necessary. Since we were at the beginning of this project, and since there was, at this time, no obstacle to re-doing the job, it seemed worth doing it right.

It was at this time that we received our first instruction regarding the French abhorrence of making a mistake. In the land *of laissez faire, joie de vivre,* and *Que sera;* where *liberté* is invoked to justify every other exception to the norm, one is not allowed to make (read that "admit") a mistake. *"On n'a pas droit à l'erreur en France"* – Odile Challe (One does not have the right to make a mistake in France) The French do not make mistakes – even if a mistake has been made, they did not make it. Admitting mistakes (and learning from them) seems to be an American value. But here we were with the drainage system in a place far from the plan. The building manager told us he would handle this delicate situation for us. We were happy, and after all, this seemed exactly the kind of thing for which we were paying him.

On our next working-vacation we inspected the misplaced drains to find that indeed they had been moved to their proper location. End of story – or so we thought.

Years had passed. The necessary additional plumbing was installed, the tile floor was laid, and the toilets set in place. Although all was not complete, the workmen began to use the toilets, against our wishes; but the use of our courtyard was not an attractive alternative. A few weeks passed. Linda first noticed the leak. It seemed to be coming through several areas of the dining room ceiling and eventually down the dining room wall. Since the plumber was on holiday, Gebbert and Linda continued their detective work and assessing of what was the most effective, yet least destructive, way to do an exploratory surgery. Cutting open the old plank ceiling of the dining room allowed them to investigate from below, rather than tearing up the tile flooring in the bathroom above.

They discovered what we had feared. The mains evacuation system, when it was corrected years ago, had been placed, but not connected properly to the rest of the evacuation system. Apparently not only are the French not allowed to make mistakes, they are not allowed to correct them either! We had a toilet that flushed into nowhere! More accurately, the toilet had been flushing these past weeks into our dining room ceiling! It was only noticed when the use became more frequent and the ceiling could absorb no more.

Gebbert sealed the connection and did the clean up without flinching. Once discovered, the actual connection was a relatively easy fix, but foul.

…on to more pleasant things.

## An update from France - Village *Fête*

Since I last wrote, at the end of August, Florensac has celebrated its Village Fête. This last weekend of August is a celebration that could be described in the quaint romantic images typical of tourist literature, that makes everyone want to rush to the south of France, or, in my preferred style, that of the benevolent curmudgeon. In which case, I hope you will still want to visit.

True, the fête is filled with local color. There are fireworks and a parade; festive lights are strung up in town. There is a "Midway" created with games of skill and small rides for little children. Most surprising is the *Grand Bal* of the festival with a very elaborate sound and light stage set up for "Las Vegas style" music groups that begin their nightly entertainment at 10 pm. Everything is very casual, but most people do dress up a notch or two above the usual – real shoes, not sandals – long pants, not shorts; ladies wear dresses, and men wear a shirt that probably needed to be ironed for the occasion; not exactly Haute Couture, but you can tell it's a special time.

These highlights are punctuated by mundane annoyances, curious quirks, and amusing small town attempts at greatness.

Two days before the fête begins the mobile carnival caravans start to arrive, bringing with them a veritable Noah's Ark of stuffed animals, plastic toys, treasures wrapped in cellophane and numerous mechanisms for little boys to launch projectiles of various sizes, shapes and colors. It is camouflaged terrorism worthy of Saddam Hussein. Parents put a firm grip on their wallets, which is inevitably relaxed by persistent cries of *"Maman…* and *Papa"*. I start waking up in the middle of the night with memories of last year's sneak attacks and bombardments. Nighttime wakening is also a form of practice for sleep deprivation and late-night disturbances, which are certain to come over the next few days for anyone (me for example) who wishes to go to bed before midnight.

The big day begins with the arrival of the *Chevalet*. This is a village totem. Florensac's totem is in the form of a horse with a "scarecrow-esque" man riding at the front and a large-busted Madame Scarecrow perched on the rear of the horse. Created like a carnival float with thousands of little red and white paper flowers, the *Chevalet* is carried by about a dozen men hidden underneath. They march along to a drumbeat. The men, half hidden on the underside, wear uniforms of white with red bandanas. At intervals they use their manpower to make the horse rear-up and spin around. There are the appropriate "Oohs" and "Aahs" from the crowd, but the more amazing thing is that this low-tech festival sport is part of a history hundreds of years old. This year there was a junior version of the *Chevalet* carried by 10-12-year olds marching behind. Passing on the tradition was clearly visible. Speaking of "behind" I have not yet found anyone to explain the significance of the horse's tail protruding from the center of the cross, symbol of the Languedoc, at the horse's rear end. I find it a bit of odd, ill-placed humor.

Exhausted by these strenuous activities everyone retires to lunch.

The next four or five evenings consist of games of chance, the fleecing of Noah's Ark, pillaging and plunder by young children who are pumped up on ice cream, cotton candy, taffy, sugar crepes and other universally recognized "health foods". Young boys arm themselves for some imaginary Armageddon. Our balcony and upper terrace seem to be prime spots for "the enemy". No doubt hidden in our flowerpots. Last year, I swept the florescent pellets from our balcony back into the street. Then, about three weeks past the village carnival, I noticed gangs of young boys assiduously searching the street gutters for ammunitions to recycle. It didn't take Sherlock Holmes to deduce that "munitions" must be running low and peace was close at hand. This year I decided to shorten the cycle by making my contribution to world peace with a direct deposit to the waste bin.

At the same time as these festivities, but separate from them, falls August 25th. This is the feast of St Louis (King Louis IX). Monsieur "Good Morning", whose real name is Louis, celebrates his patron's day by baking *Oriellettes* ("Elephant Ear" fried sugar pastries). He distributes them throughout the village. We are on his list. So, we awake to a fresh batch of pastries baked and placed in a sack at our door by our 91-year-old friend. Some nourishment to hold body and soul together as we ward off the perils of pugnacious, pre-pubescent pranksters.

**September Scenes of Village Life**

The major tourist traffic made its grand exit right on schedule the last weekend of August. No doubt, the beginning of the school year drew them all back to reality. Tourists, caravan trailers, and traffic departed to make room on the roads for the local farmers' tractors. The *vendanges* began in Mid-September. The *vendanges* is serious grape harvesting and intensive work for two to three weeks. Everyone prays that there will be no rain until October. Rain at the end of the growing period (I am told) reduces the sugar content and alcohol potential of the grapes. This year it rained.

Rain also makes for muddy vineyards. Many vignerons still pick their grapes by hand. Workers place the grapes in large baskets, and then pile them high in small trailers to be taken away. We can hear the earliest of the tractors leave about 4:00 am for the fields. Days are assigned for different grape varieties -- One day for Merlot, another for Cabernet, another for Syrah etc.

Ordinarily I think of the French as "organizationally challenged". Seldom (I try to avoid saying never) do things start (or end) on time. This is the land of the unexpected closing, the *"Fermeture Exceptional"*, which is only discovered after you have made the trip to the shop. Getting from here to there is never (truly, never) a straight shot, and the directions, for one who is lost, are only clear, after you have arrived. But the vendange is amazingly well organized, and people seem to follow the rules -- well, most of the time.

Over the years, some vineyards have been prepared, planted and pruned to accommodate modern technical equipment. These fields are picked by machines two stories tall, which look like they were imported from central casting of "Stars Wars". There is a buzz of activity throughout the village as most conversations eventually turn to some aspect of the harvest. You can also see and feel the grape juice sticking to your shoes and crackling under the tires where the tractors with grape-ladened wagons drive through town on the way to the Domaine or the Cave Cooperative for processing.

Our social calendar is beginning to show signs of a gradual assimilation into French life. Next week Linda resumes her English tutoring of one of the children in the village, and we are making the transition from those short *"Bon Jour"* sidewalk pleasantries to invitations for *apéritives* / aperitifs.

The *apéritive* invitations have come from two French families, and we have hosted one on our terrace at rue Molière. This French version of "happy hour" is a challenge for our developing abilities in the *lingua franca*. It lasts for about an hour and a half to two hours – a drink or two helps. There is much hand gesturing and much patience on the part of all. In the process, we manage to learn some local history, a little of the local lore about our house, and we can practice our French with these new friends. Now, I don't expect much sympathy from you, but these simple social events require all the verbal skills, stamina, and endurance we can muster.

Two of our *apéritive* events were part of the purchase of some fine French furniture from a family in town. Our longtime friend, 90-year-old Madame Donatien, asked me one day, if we might be interested in some old furniture. Her son and daughter-in-law had some furniture that belonged to the daughter-in-law's great-grand parents and the grandchildren did not want it. During *apéritives*, we were shown the furniture. Next day, I made our offer, and they made their counter offer over the telephone. Yesterday, the family delivered their beautiful walnut bedroom set, style Henri II over 100 years old, and a second armoire that is two hundred years old. We admired them for one day and then covered them up to protect them from the construction dust.

We have a favorite p*otager* / vegetable stand that we frequent in town. Madame runs this business out of her living room window. She often rounds-off the total for purchases in favor of her clients. This makes for a few more fruits or vegetables for the client and a few less *centimes* in her pocket, but much good will. The produce is straight from the garden with little ceremony and no packaging. I tell Linda that I have purchased enough French dirt on Madame Potager's vegetables to start a garden of my own. Recently, I was looking for some fresh figs. During the height of the season, there are plenty of figs free for the taking from branches hanging over village garden walls. In our former lives this would be unacceptable. But we learned of this from some rather respectable neighbors, "Take them" they tell us. However, late in the season, I must resort to buying fresh figs to eat with my Roquefort. Unfortunately, there were none that day. Next day I returned, and Madame Potager pulled me aside. She had a handful of figs and whispered some advice while gesturing in the direction of the other customer sorting through the lettuces. "Buy them now, because she will take all that are left!" I purchased six and got eight in my sack.

On the Anniversary of September 11th there were remembrances across France. Two villagers thought to ask us if we had had family or friends injured or killed in the attacks. And we had some B&B guests who finally made their trip to France. Their original trip had been postponed because of flight cancellations at that time last year.

This year they enjoyed le petit jardin de l'âme in a more finished, but not yet completed state. They considered adopting Gebbert to help them with their renovation project in the USA and in their thank you note sent greetings to Guy Noël (the name on the cement mixer, which until last week, was a permanent resident in our someday-it-will-be-a dining room). We seem to attract a very special B&B clientele. They seem to enjoy being a part of the creation of our dream.

I can now send them a note to say that, with no regrets, Guy Noel is recently among the dearly departed. Guy, along with the last of our gross construction materials – scaffolding, wheel barrel, cement blocks, "re-bar", dry wall, wooden planks, miscellaneous empty cans, a 50-gallon water drum, and an odd assortment of levers, crowbars, winches and wrenches -- has been trucked off to some other happy home; I care not where.

We are not finished, but at last, we are on to some finer things. You know … the scraping and cleaning of corners, and bumps, and rough spots that the workers just don't seem to notice, but are a necessary cleanup before finishes are applied. We must find a *carreleur* / tile man once again. Our preferred *carreleur* said he might be available to do the job sometime, eight months from now, in April (2003). I think this makes number seven or eight *carreleurs* that we have been through in this project. This even exceeds our list of plumbers (five). Nevertheless, I remind myself that these days are soon to pass. We are now putting a coat (or two) of linseed oil on the window frames and polyurethane on the ceiling beams. The old floor tiles in our master bedroom need to be waxed after we scrape off the drops of plaster and cement and other debris that has been left behind. All the leaks have been found and the plumbing works- Hurrah! Things are looking good. We now have a "to-do" list for Gebbert that fits on one page and shows him that we are nearly finished. He has another job lined up for November with another renovation here in Florensac. It is a *bergerie* / shepherd's house and courtyard. We have seen the "before" state of the buildings. It is a challenge equal to, or greater than, our own. We make a joke with Gebbert that he is very selective about the projects he takes on. He says, "I only take on the impossible. You can get anybody to do the possible."

For vacation, Gebbert plans to take a break and return to his "first love" as a street musician singing at the local markets for a few weeks. Have we been touched by an angel, or what?

## An Update from France – October/November

It has been two months, nearly three, since I have written an Update from France. *Tempus Fugit!* October has come and gone and so has this month of November. I am reminded of John Mortimer's reference to the playwright Christopher Fry

*"It is the law of script writing that scenes get shorter and the action speeds up toward the end. In childhood, the afternoon spreads out for 'years'. For the old, the years flicker past like the briefest of afternoons. Sometimes it seems that we are having breakfast every five minutes."*
-John Mortimer, *Summer of A Dormouse*

Do I dare say we are almost finished -- again? We have been saying that for so long that one of our friends in the English-speaking community told me recently that he had heard a joke. After he had my attention, and I responded with appropriate curiosity, he smiled and said, "Someone told me you were finished with your house – I knew they must be kidding." We ARE nearly finished. This time we know it is true. Our aching bodies tell us so. Linda has spent way too many hours cleaning plaster, cement and years of accumulated crud from the old terra cotta tile on the floor of our someday-it-will-be-a master bedroom suite. And I have spent less, but still way too many hours filling in cracks, camouflaging broken tiles and otherwise covering up the damage done by workmen during the renovation. There are many more months of cleaning and decoration ahead for us, but the construction seems over for now. One by one the workers have gone. The house and garden are ours once again. Nevertheless, I do have one or two "Tales from This Old House".

As the plumber made his departure, he said, at the front door *"Avec plaisir je dis au revoir* / With pleasure I say goodbye". His smile had *"double entendre"* written all over it. Linda smiled back and said *"Moi aussi."* Each knew what the other meant.

The electrician has not quite finished his work, but he is no longer impeding progress. We commemorated a one-year anniversary with him on his recent visit. In some way, this delay is a good thing, since we have now discovered some mysterious power outages! There seems to be a pattern here. The plumber announced to us that he was finished, and expected full payment immediately. We pointed out to him that we had not even turned on the water to see if things worked. As we completed our preliminary tests, it was clear that we had seven leaks. Some were minor some were more important, but they were all leaks. We were happy that we still had some financial leverage in our pocket to draw him back and make the repairs. Now the electrician thinks he is nearly finished and wants his payment, but *Quelle dommage*! Even writing this Update on the computer becomes a harrowing task since the power could go out at any moment. Although our computer is protected from power **surges**, we are not protected from French electricians. Another one of God's little exercises for me in "powerlessness"? – I THINK NOT.

Early in October, we took a break from construction. We took a day long horse and carriage ride with some friends. It was enjoyable research for our future B&B guests. This carriage tour travels the back roads to four local domaines for wine tasting and stops for a picnic lunch in the garrigue near an old abandoned church. It was a great way to enjoy a cool, clear, sunny autumn day, and remember why it is we came to France.

During early November long-time family friends visited. We were once again able to be tourists for a day or two taking in a Mediterranean seaside lunch and a visit to one of the domaines of Florensac for a tasting of some wine we had had the previous night at dinner just down the road at Auberge Trois Pins. Although <u>Rouge No.1</u> is not an exotic vintage year from a Bordeaux Chateau, it was our favorite. Monsieur and Madame were generous with their time and their wine. We may have caught Madame a little bit unprepared. She seemed to have forgotten to put her teeth in that day. On the other hand, was it just south of France casual?

The FCTU (French Children's Terrorism Unit) has found yet another game to play within earshot of our balcony at *Cœur de Village*. It seems that the narrow walls of the Allée in front of our house are ideal for playing "Tambourine". The game is a bit like handball, but played with tennis balls and – yes, you guessed it -- that percussion instrument meant for gypsies! So far, I have returned the tennis balls that have come lobbing up onto our balcony. However, this is not a gratuitous gesture. It is an opportunity for me to practice my French. With curmudgeon-like sternness I pick up the offending ball, look down (I like this elevated position for effect) and make a solemn pronouncement *"Mes enfants, il est temps de jouer devant chez toi* / My children it is time to go play in front of your house." A useful phrase not taught in standard French 101.

This time of year is becoming my favorite time of year. Although the rain begins, it is also the time of year when the village is most quiet and the streets most clean. The children play more often inside, and God does his part to wash down the streets with the rain. (I am sure the feminists will pardon this reference to God as masculine, since it also implies that God seldom helps with the cleaning and He does not listen to me most of the time.)

And so, it goes. Day by day, France is becoming home for us. Using an analogy from gastronomy, I might describe it in this way. For Linda life in France was "love at first bite". For me, well – life in France is an acquired taste.

## An Acquired Taste

My attempt to "acquire a taste" for France was reflected in my occasional glimmers of hope, when, there was a continued realization that the France of my retirement dream, and the France of my day to day life were so very, depressingly different. In some ways, the closer we came to finish our construction project, and the long-anticipated relief from the day-to-day hassles with workmen, the more I had time to notice the world around me.

There were, it is true, some moments that resembled the dream: A lovely spring day in the country, quiet moments in our courtyard, the occasional courtesy and unexpected little gifts of home grown produce from a growing list of elderly acquaintances in the village. There were some pleasant times together for Linda and me, but it was clear that she and I were no longer of one mind and heart on this life in France, as we once had been. For me, the pleasing moments were overshadowed by, what I came to identify, as generalized incivility and passive aggressive behaviors which surrounded us and to which I responded with a constant watchfulness. I had been conditioned by my new environment to be a sentinel, on constant guard, watchful to protect our space, our peace, and our pocket book. I had never felt the need to live in a state of constant defense.

My past life had not been a sheltered life. I was accustomed to the perceived risks of living in "the big city". And, I had often sorted the complexities of corporate politics. I was, in general, and by professional training, an accurate observer of human behavior. Being alert to the various dynamics of human interaction was not foreign to me. But never had I found it something that influenced my everyday existence so completely. In the past, I had enjoyed living my life in a spirit of trust and mutual respect, until I was given reason to doubt. Here, I was experiencing the opposite.

What I am about to tell you next, happened in the summer months soon after our move to *le petit jardin*, but I include it now because it illustrates a type of interaction that became increasingly intolerable. It is one example of a style of interaction typical of our life in

France. It was particularly difficult during the autumn of 2002 and well into 2003.

As you know, I looked forward to the move from *Cœur de Village* to *le petit jardin*, not only because I wished to live in the home we dreamed of, but also because the street and its residents on rue Molière were quieter in their ways than at *Cœur de Village*. We had over the years of our preparatory vacations sensed the beginning of some friendships with a few of the life-long residents on the street. I hoped, perhaps, that our most turbulent times would be left behind at *Cœur de Village* and that a quiet, more genteel life awaited us on rue Molière.

Shortly after we settled in at *le petit jardin*, new neighbors arrived. They had purchased a small home down the street and did some modest renovation of the space. Within weeks of their arrival I discovered that I was often awakened during the late-night hours -- past midnight -- to the sounds of television programs and late-night movie orchestral themes. Initially, I thought that perhaps this was just an occasional oversight on their part, and would pass. But eventually, I concluded that this was becoming a pattern; the sounds of their entertainment drifting in to my bedroom were loud enough to wake me from a sound sleep. One night, it was a late, late movie of biblical proportions with Cecil B. DeMille style crowd scenes and sound track crescendos that finally roused me from my bed. I put on my clothes, went down to the street, and knocked on their door.

"Rap, rap, rap". But apparently, they could not hear me over the blare of the television dialogue or the climactic sound track. Again, with firmness of intention, I knocked, "Rap Rap Rap". I realized that if the neighborhood were not already awake, surely, my "rapping" was now enough to wake the dead. Monsieur came to the window at the *premiere étage* / second floor.

In the process of their move into their new home and the occasional *"Bonjour"*, I realized that this couple spoke very good English. Therefore, I used the language in which I was more confident. In English I said, "Monsieur, I can hear your television in my bedroom."

His response; "Oh, and what were they saying?"

I quickly searched my brain for a diplomatic response, since my first reaction would probably have been inflammatory. I simply repeated my statement, giving him a second opportunity for a more neighborly reply. "Sir, I can hear your television in my bedroom and it is past midnight."

"And what would you like me to do?"

His tone would not win him the Nobel Peace Prize, but I took him at his word and thought of this as a starting point, since apparently, he was asking for my advice.

I said, "Please close your window and reduce the volume on your television."

I never expected him to close his window; it was a warm summer's night. But I thought it wise to ask for more than I expected, to give him some room for negotiation.

With a harrumph, he said he would reduce the volume on the television. I returned to my bed and within minutes realized that I had been defeated. For, if the volume had in fact been altered, its effect was imperceptible. As I lay there, I considered whether I should press my point now, or wait for another night, since it was sure to come. I decided that there was no better moment than now. I dressed again, and returned to the street. "Rap, Rap, Rap"

This time, the lady of the house appeared at the window. The dialogue began in the same way. But she went on, to sermonize, from the pulpit of her balcony, observing that I seemed to be the only one on the street who was having a problem when they watched their television. Taking a deep breath, I gave reason one more try and said, "That you are watching your television is not a problem, but I should not have to listen to your television in my bedroom." I knew that I was, in fact, the only one who voiced a complaint. But I knew others on the street were troubled by it.

In general, my experience of the French has been that they will not speak out directly to an offence or offender, but will complain to each other. I had heard just such complaints as part of a short conversation between two other neighbors a few days earlier, under this same window. The topic of conversation was the late-night television and the volume. The discussion in the street, on that day, was intentionally loud enough to be heard by the new owners, inside, if they cared to listen. However, on this night, I was alone in the street and sensing defeat.

It was at this moment that I heard a small voice, from a young woman, the neighbor on the other side of our house. My attention had been so focused on the window above, that I failed to notice that a comrade had joined me in the street! She spoke up in French saying, "Madame, I too can hear your television in my bedroom, it is intolerable." And as if by magic, a third voice appeared from the balcony across the street. A simple *"Oui"* came out of the darkness. It was Madame Blonde adding emphatic support with a sonorous, single syllable.

At that moment I felt "I have arrived"! The neighbors were supporting me in a common cause, and I was no longer the new kid on the block. The woman in the window above said nothing. She closed her window with a theatrical flair and the sound disappeared from her TV. I smiled and gave a big *"Merci*, b*on nuit"* to my comrades. I went back to bed. The night was calm. But now I could not sleep, I was so excited!

Before we proceed, I should note that it was necessary, a few weeks later to have this midnight conversation yet one more time. During this second confrontation, I did not have the visible support of the other neighbors, but I had a sense that they were lending moral support from behind their shutters.

During the autumn and winter months of 2002, I became increasingly depressed about this way of life in France. Yes, occasionally I was buoyed by a momentary success, and occasional pleasantries; but the positives were fleeting and infrequent. My everyday contact with *la vie en france* was, for me, a daily dose of despair. It seemed, I lived my life, among tricksters, dodgers and opportunists; those who would take advantage at every turn.

I enjoyed our growing number of English friends but found that these relationships, which seemed a better fit for me, also highlighted what was lacking in my experiences with the French. I seriously regretted the investment we had made in creating our life of retirement in France. My growing sense of despair began to include suicidal thoughts from time to time.

I had hoped that life in France would all be better once the construction was finished. For most of the two years since our move to France, this hope was something I had held out ahead of me. But challenges like the one above with our new neighbors, made me realize that even when the renovation was finished, life in France might well be the same as before. The closer we came to finishing, the clearer it became that the quality of life in France that I sought would remain elusive – perhaps unattainable.

> *I had a dream my life would be different from this hell I am living, so different from what it seemed. Now life has killed the dream I dreamed.*
> -Victor Hugo

I write in the journal:

> November 2002
>
> > In some ways things have improved. Perhaps it is the effect of the medication since I see no appreciable change in people's behaviors around me. And for my behaviors, I work consciously, searching for the positive, and look forward to the move to le petit jardin de l'âme. But I must admit that there is a growing attitude forming, that I cannot, I will not, continue to live in this environment indefinitely. When we move to rue Molière there is the potential for a more secluded living space, less penetrable by the noise and clutter and garbage. I hope that I can live in this semi-secluded condition and bolster myself to make the necessary forays into the streets for brief periods to do necessary errands. This is not what I had hoped for; not

the integration into French life I expected of myself. It is a way of surviving, not a way of living.

I have stopped fighting with the workmen, they are impossible, arrogant, and soon, a passing chapter in our lives. I hope now only to be rid of them. For the moment, I have stopped expecting to develop any significant relationships in the village. I expect nothing of them or myself beyond a few superficial *"Bon jours"* and a civil smile. The elder, more established neighbors on rue Molière are pleasant and welcoming. But, in their 80's and 90's, they are a reminder of a way of life, *la vie en France*, which is passing away.

I am grateful that we have discovered some English-speaking friends. There is the potential for growing friendships with them based on common interests. This is a bright spot in an otherwise dismal area of finding people with whom I can have a decent conversation.

The recent request by some in this group for a traditional Christmas Lessons and Carols service is a refreshing surprise. I am happy to have been asked to preach and have only the familiar anxieties related to "doing a good job". This is a joyful area of work for me. As I become more "out of the closet" as a clergyman, I find a significant new inner tension developing. It is difficult to engage whole heartedly in the role of pastor and at the same time know that I am haunted by recurring thoughts of suicide as a way out of what I see as an intolerable life in France. In theory there is always another option, but I do not see a realistic option out of France.

To sell, and return to the USA is not a realistic possibility; the financial loss would be horrendous, not to mention the difficulties of starting over again professionally, since, in these two years, my licenses and certifications have expired. Our visas do not allow for employment here, we did not anticipate needing employment. But any significant change – to move anywhere -- at this point, would require an influx of cash to re-establish our life elsewhere. While we have enough to live on, our investment portfolio has taken a significant hit in the past two years and needs time to recover. And, most importantly, we are not together on this. Admitting defeat is one thing, difficult to swallow but sometimes necessary. But, the thought of fleeing and absorbing the total cost in the form of a significant financial loss and reduced standard of living makes me furious. Feeling trapped, defeated, and angry wasn't exactly what I had in mind for retirement.

Of course, we expected tension in our life as husband and wife during this time. I believe that we were prepared for the stress on our marriage that was to come with a major life change and the renovation project. But, I expected that in the end we would succeed. I now believe that creating the life we hoped for is not possible and we will fail. There is something incongruous about trying to revive our intimate life together, while at the same time I have an unspeakable "way out" which I cannot share with you. The thought that we have sunk our entire retirement dream into this life in France troubles me greatly. We grow further apart not only in how we see the world of our life in France but also in how we view each other. I am sorry for this deception, but if I surrender my suicide thoughts to you, I place you in a difficult situation, and I lose one of my necessary options for coping currently. To change course seems unwise, yet I find it increasingly impossible to work toward a future here. This is the death of a dream.

*I always admired those who let their nightmares free.*
*Most of mine I keep secret in the Diary,*
*not always willing to share the doubts, fears, visions,*
*in my eagerness to overcome and conquer them*
*for the sake of passionate affirmation.*
-Anais Nin

Correspondence with family and friends continued to focus on the positive while acknowledging some of the more expected, and humorous aspects of adjustment. And in fact, attention to the details of finishing the house was a task in which I could lose myself for hours: a pleasant, and necessary escape from life around us.

At the approach of our second year of holidays, except for the English Service of Lessons and Carols, we were still without real holiday celebrations. In general, things were a little dreary, again, not too different from our first year. We were not yet ready to celebrate. We were neither physically settled -- we had not unpacked -- nor were we psychologically settled. The last of the workmen were still laying tiles on our living room floor. To me, it was a symbolic act as they worked their way across the living room floor and in the direction of the front door. Linda had the perseverance to watch nearly every tile put in place. It seemed that having the floor finished and the last workmen gone would be our Christmas present to each other.

**Thanksgiving**

> Happy Thanksgiving! We realized this morning that it was Thanksgiving but no Macy's parade and no TODAY with Katie and Matt, Al and Ann on NBC. No real "turkey-day" here in France – maybe next year.
>
> I am taking a break between touchups here at rue Molière. Most workers have gone but there is a lot of detail work still to do before we move in. The last few days I spent in the master bedroom closet, doing a decorative "French wash" on the walls (it is a good place to practice for the larger rooms), waxing the floor, doing the baseboard, and finishing the door. All this before we put in closet organizers, and hang our clothes, that have been packed for nearly two years. Linda has spent time making the stone surround for the gas fireplace in the living room. We have set the gas burning fireplace inside the old original fireplace in the living room and it needs some attention to make it fit properly and tastefully. She is working also on refinishing an old *"port-manteau* / Hall tree" which we purchased. When finished, it will be a functional, as well as a decorative, cover-up for the electric circuit breaker box,

that for some reason, could not be placed in the garage but had to be placed -- where else? -- In our living room! She will hinge the *port-manteau* to the wall so that we can open it like a door if needed to get at the box behind it. And so, that's how our days are spent ! We have one young fellow, Adib, who comes back as we need him. He is good at work that is more detailed, so we use him for minor patching and painting of primer on the walls. We found that the other workmen were just too careless, which resulted in more paint on the freshly cleaned wood beams than on the walls.

Our annual Christmas letter for 2002 was less than cheery, but we did attempt to include some of the delightful experiences of life in France. It seemed that, even from our little corner of the world we were aware that the global retrospective on 2002 was also not all that great. Was our Christmas letter a reflection of our personal experiences alone? Or had the new millennium simply begun with a bust?

## Christmas 2002

> le petit jardin de l'âme
> 10 rue Molière Florensac 34510 France
> www.petitjardin.com
>
> We are a little late in sending our Christmas greetings this year. We figure that you will excuse us since we have only recently recovered from the euphoria that came when the last workman departed from the construction site – soon to be our home! Still, we hope this will reach you sometime during these twelve days of Christmas.        .
>
> We are well, and continue to adjust to our life in France. In addition to the seemingly endless cross-cultural surprises, we are also adjusting to a world economy that has reduced the US$ to par with the € Euro and significantly reduced the value of our stock portfolio – again. I care not to remember that this year was the year when it became more

expensive for us to live in France. We have lost our exchange rate advantage.

I recently read a review of the year 2002 in the end-of-the year edition of *The Economist*. It described the year 2002 as "surprisingly good" – and then went on to put this news in the context of how much worse things might have been. Perhaps this type of "optimism" illustrates a real change in our collective consciousness when we identify "good" as the absence of something worse. No room here for a sermon but, sadly, I do think they are on to something. .

2002 has not been the easiest of years –again -- but nothing that cannot be managed by a little Prozac, Xanax, psychotherapy, a sense of humor, patience, patience and more patience. The last three coping mechanisms more often found in Linda than "moi".

We have been fortunate this year to survive living nearly two years of "under construction". We look forward to a new year of life in France that begins to resemble the life we came to live. We have received inquiries for summer B&B reservations and, as soon as we clean the construction dust from the kitchen, we will be ready to prepare a *"Table d'Hôte"* for our guests in the garden. During this past year, we have been recipients of generous hospitality from several new friends – many English retirees – and one local French family. One November meal we will share with you. Our Florensac neighbor invited us to a special lunch. The *pièce de résistance* was the *Escargots Florensacois* - snails prepared in a way unique to Florensac – a thick rich sauce of walnuts, ham, mint, and spices from the garrigue. The entire meal was a delight, but the escargots (all 350 of them) were the centerpiece. They had been gathered by hand on the hillside and fed flour and spices for one month to clean them before they came to their glorious end in our large soup bowls. Our lunch lasted for 5 hours with local wine, cheese and a dessert made by 91-year-old Monsieur "Good Morning". This afternoon reminded us of why we came to France!

In early December, Linda kept our families updated on the progression of the floodwaters from the Hérault River. In the end we, and the town, remained dry. However, it was our first time to see the river flood the plain and to see the simple but masterful engineering that keeps the Hérault River away from our door, all-be-it, not by much. The oldest members of the village cannot remember a time when the village ever flooded. They went to the dike more as a curiosity than out of any real concern. They advised Linda that this was "*comme d'habitude* / as usual" and not serious. It did provide a real conversation opportunity for Linda who made frequent trips to the dike and met several of her favorite little old men along way.

Another first for us was what may become an Annual English Christmas Carol Service. A few months ago, some friends asked if I would be interested in "helping out" with such a service. This evolved into a wonderful cooperative experience and my "outing" as an Episcopal Priest. My first Sermon here in France was to a gathering of about 150 English and a few French. It was a grand success and the local French Roman Catholic Pastor, from whom we borrowed the church, asked to have my sermon translated for his congregation. In the process, we also found one retired Anglican clergy and a priest from the Old Catholic Church who are interested in working together. There were several Anglicans as well who were "pleased to see that there was an 'English Vicar' in the area". Who knows where this will lead?

We continue to write our monthly "Updates from France" – short summaries of our adjustment to life in France and the trials and tribulations of renovation of "*Cette Vielle Maison* / This Old House" Several people have hinted that we should publish. We are considering what that might involve. Contacts for publishers, editors, etc. will be gratefully received. Who knows where this will lead?

*The Economist*'s review of the year 2002 and its intriguing point-of-view observed that at least there were no terrorist attacks on the scale of September 11, 2001. That seems a strange measure of "a good year". But it did make me think of how fortunate we are here at le petit jardin de l'âme. Our Moroccan, Muslim *carreleur* / tile man brought us a plate of sweets from his family's feast at the end of Ramadan. And, although he speaks no English, wished us a "Happy Christmas" before he left on Christmas Eve. That, and the fact that the floor looks beautiful, seemed to me a good sign for a better 2003

# Of Light and Shadow in 2003

### A Heart Warming Experience

Our big event(s) in the New Year were not at all on our "to-do list". January was the month when we got to know the medical care system in France. All is fine now, and we can look back in relief.

On 15 January, I took Linda to the emergency room with her heart beating a lively 240 a minute. French signage being what it is, I entered the ER via the exit ramp but *c'est la vie*, we were there. Conditioned as we were by the medical system in the USA, we were shocked to discover that in France they ask for your symptoms first and not your insurance carrier. After five days at the new, first class, Central Hospital at Béziers, Linda returned home and then followed up with an overnight stay for treatment at Montpellier Hospital on 29 January. An amazing arterial probe that lasers away the problem has cured her atrial flutter. While, under the benefits of a sedative, one can watch the procedure on a monitor – or at least Linda did. It was the first TV she has seen in two years – and she was the star! The atrial fibrillation will continue to be managed by medication as it was before.

Linda accomplished her enforced random research of French hospitals with her French/English dictionary under her one arm and her medical files from the USA under the other. I must say that our French must have shown signs of improvement. She was confident of her conversations in French and English with the doctors. In addition, I was surprised that in recovery, in her semi-anesthetized state, Linda told me, in French, *J'ai besoin rester tranquille et droit* / I need to lay still and straight.

The medical staff was wonderful and the medical care A+. After two years of our experiences with French workers during the renovation, I had my fears. Thank heavens; French cardiologists, nurses and medical staff instill more confidence than French plumbers, electricians, roofers, tilers, etc!

Of course, the hospital visits were filled with a few cross-cultural surprises. Linda emailed family and friends with these bits of cross-culture trivia:

> If you are ever dizzy – and in France – the idiom to use is *"tomber dans les pommes /* to fall into the apples". Of course, you could also use the generic, "malaise", but it is not as colorful.

> Hospital meals were not bad, but it did make me appreciate Val's home cooking and colorful presentations. When my last meal at Central Hospital of Montpellier arrived, the lunch menu said I was to have 25 cl of red wine. Hum! I had heard about this practice, but where was mine? ...Not on my tray. Perhaps the server was coming back with it. But after several minutes hearing the cart continuing to move down the hall, it seemed unlikely. Since I was ready to go home, dressed, and feeling quite frisky and curious, I went and asked for it, only to find out that they give the wine to" les *hommes pas les femmes /* the men and not the women". I got mine anyway, and I'm sorry to say it was the most awful wine I've ever tasted. I guess medicinal value has nothing to do with quality.

> I'm home from the treatment that apparently has stopped my atrial flutter forever, but probably not the atrial fibrillation. Medical treatments are never as easy as they seem beforehand, so the little wire that ran up from my groin to my heart and burned strategic spots in the heart was a bit more uncomfortable than I expected. And the aftermath of the anesthesia quite unpleasant, but now all is forgotten, and I feel great.

> As a connoisseur of hospitals, I must say that my favorite was Béziers. The building was beautiful, and posted on the back of each patient door and throughout the hospital was a mission statement about what patients could expect from their caregivers. On the back of the door at Central Hospital of Montpellier was a notice warning you to lock up any valuables in the safe provided for you at admission, because they

weren't safe in your room. Welcome to the big city. I sent everything home with Val.

People in Florensac were very supportive during the hospitalizations. In a village of this size, people know when you drop out of sight for a few days. The hairdresser noticed that she had not seen Linda on her normal walks past the shop. The people at the bakery wondered why Monsieur was getting the baguette today, Madame always gets the breakfast bread, etc. It doesn't take long before word gets around. Of the many nice greetings, one was particularly special. After her return from the hospital, Linda was walking down one of the village streets. The 14-year-old son of Madame Dupont, met her. With the charm of a fine young man and the tenderness of a child, he asked how Linda was feeling and gave her three kisses on the cheeks as the French do with their friends here in the south -- a touch of graciousness.

Eventually, we returned to our normal routine; cleaning, cleaning, and more cleaning. When we were not cleaning construction dust from every nook, cranny, beam and floor tile, we were making miscellaneous repairs and finishing the work left behind by our recently departed "artisans". Their sins of omission had been many. Eventually, it seemed that we were faced with the law of diminishing returns. Where we had attempted to hold them accountable for good work in one area, we experienced breakage, damage, or carelessness in another area. We had come to the conclusion that sometimes it is best just to get the bull out of the china shop.

Our work allowed us to make the space our own, and we were doing the things we do best. We are experts at camouflaging imperfections and creating ambiance. Our B&B guests were to arrive in early March. Therefore, it was necessary to finish the last of the guest rooms. In addition, the two guest rooms that were finished earlier needed to be freshened up. We made progress in setting up our home office. And the garden was, at last, looking like a garden. Then, there was the task of getting the kitchen functional ... and on, and on. Qualitatively, there was such a difference now that we are here working side by side. Often, we would go about our tasks separately and "meet for lunch". There was now a chance for calm to return to this space, with the workmen gone.

*The ninety and nine are with dreams, content,*
*but the hope of the world made new,*
*is the hundredth man who is grimly bent*
*on making those dreams come true.*
-Edgar Allan Poe

## An update from France – March

At the end of March in Languedoc, we find ourselves well past the crocus and tulips of early spring. The white/pink blossoms of the almond trees that brighten the hillsides in early March are now in their later days. In addition, the petals from the flowering plum trees in Florensac are scattered about the village streets like so much confetti from Carnival. The first signs of leafing out of the vines in the fields can be seen if you look closely. However, more important than all of this is that this spring, we actually have a garden at le petit jardin de l'âme! Admittedly, it is a young garden and needs time for maturing, but our solanum survived the winter and much abuse during the renovation. It nearly reaches fully across the beam at the edge of the covered part of the garden and by summer will have wrapped itself around the wrought iron railing outside our guest bedroom, just as we planned. Yesterday I gave our rosemary its "spring haircut" and have flavor enough to tie into bunches and share with our friends.

I will pass over our unsuccessful horticultural experiments and garden mortalities to simply say that the garden centers are very pleased to see us return this spring.

One of the signs of "upscale" development in the area is the growing number of garden centers. When we first arrived, it was hard to find a retail nursery. In the past two years, this business has taken off, and we have several fine options available nearby. On a smaller local scale, we were saddened in the autumn to see the closure – due to retirement -- of the only florist shop in Florensac. But voila! Two new florists have sprung up at the center of town!

During this time for spring pruning of the vineyards, Linda, while on one of her daily "promenades", asked one of the vignerons if we could have some of the sarments (cuttings from the grape vines) for our barbeque. The Vigneron – whom we call "Mr. Rogers" – gladly gave them to us, since, he had too many and would only burn them in a bonfire. However, he warned us that these cuttings would be good for NEXT summer's barbeque after they dried. We were happy to take them and trim them into bundles for individual use next year. What we would pay *beaucoup* bucks for in a boutique in Chicago is free for the asking here in Florensac.

The village is a bustle of spring renovation activities. The Old Village Post Office and Treasury are under renovation. Word on the street is that someone from Paris has purchased it and is renovating it for residential use. Three houses on rue General Fraisse have begun renovations of their facades in the last month. The dust is awful, but the attention to those old village houses is encouraging. There seems to be a new restaurant opening in town – hurrah! In addition, one of our stand-byes, *La Noria*, seems to have had a good year: they are remodeling. I am happy to say, that this year, we content ourselves with relatively minor decorating tasks rather than the trials of renovation.

Around mid-March we began to eat our lunches al fresco, as weather permitted. By this time of the month, lunch in the sun can be enjoyed most days. Linda lit the first fire for a lunchtime barbeque in our garden today. Evenings are too cool yet for outdoor dining, but two nearby *Auberges* provide wonderful fireside evening meals. And some of our favorite restaurants in nearby *Marseillan* are beginning to re-open after their long winter's nap.

Our life here seems so much different from the tensions of the larger world around us. Of course, there is talk of the war in Iraq, but it seems removed from this rural life. The French seem to distinguish between the policies of the Bush Administration and the many Americans who have a different view. We have felt no personal incrimination or discrimination. We do find it interesting reading, comparing the French, English, and American versions of the news events from their individual news sources. We have attempted only limited conversation about the war in one of our French classes in the home of Madeline Le Point here in town. But, we have had several lively discussions among English friends in the area.

We have decided to wait until the month of May to make our move from the little house at rue General Fraisse to our home at rue Molière. In part, this decision was since, with the workmen gone we now had time on our side to prepare our home, as we wanted it. We also decided that it seemed an extravagance to pour heat into the large house to take away the winter's chill, only to want to cool it down again for the approaching summer. During informal consultations with the neighbors, they agreed. So, we are close, but not yet settled into the way of life we came to live. It is clearly within reach, and we spend most of our days at rue Molière trimming, painting, polishing, putting up shelves and, at last, unpacking boxes which came from Chicago more than two years ago. While unpacking boxes of some of our better china, glassware and silver, I felt a bit like an archeologist discovering a lost way of life, buried since our arrival. It was much like the beginning of a fairy tale. *Il était une fois* / Once upon a time.

I look forward to moving from "limbo" to le petit jardin de l'âme.

## Doin' the Dustbin Shuffle

The French call them *Poubelles*, our English friends call them Dustbins. I prefer to call them Garbage-containers, because that is what they contain. Euphemisms can be so misleading. Dustbins do, perhaps, contain some dust, and a whole lot more. *Poubelles* certainly do not contain Eugène René Poubelle (1831-1907), for whom the French named them. Whatever the name, dustbins and *poubelles* contain garbage! The discarded remnants of food and personal hygiene, which we do not wish to have in our homes, we put in -- the garbage container.

In what follows, there is, perhaps, more than you ever cared to know about garbage collection in France. But, this is not about garbage collection. It is about a way of life.

One of the changes I was anticipating in our move to *le petit jardin* was an escape from the daily sight of the communal *poubelles* at the collection point, which was within ten feet of the front door at *Cœur de Village*. In theory, the change from these communal garbage containers were made sometime during 2002. Under the old communal garbage collection system, garbage for the residents of the street was brought, *ad libitum*, to three, large, communal *poubelles* across the street. Sacks of everyone's daily refuse filled the bins, often to overflowing. It was not unusual for sacks containing discarded foodstuffs to fall, or be placed, outside the bins onto the pavement. The bins were foul. And carelessness invited numerous wandering dogs to raid the area, breaking open the sacks and scattering the contents along the street. Most of the neighbors had developed immunity to picking up the garbage. I could not resist. It became a daily chore. A very unpleasant daily chore made tolerable, in part, because it was to be temporary.

We were told that new European Community regulations would soon require a change to this system. When the new system of individual garbage bins was introduced, we welcomed the change. Under the new system, an individual household received two domestic-sized *poubelles*; one for recyclable plastics, paper, etc., and one for everything else. In theory, these containers were kept in the individual homes until the evening before garbage collection. Twice each week the garbage was collected, and once each week for the recyclables. The place of the old overflowing communal bins was to become the collection point where residents placed their individual bins on the night before pick-up. Then, "as soon as possible", the next morning the bins were to be retrieved by their owners and returned to their individual homes. It seemed a surprisingly simple, sane, and sanitary system.

When we first received our individual *poubelles*, their size seemed a bit problematic for our little house at *Cœur de Village*. They were much bigger than we expected for two persons. But, we found a way to make them fit and convinced ourselves that with diligent cleaning they would not be an odiferous problem. And for our little home, it worked. But, within a few weeks of the inauguration of the new system, the collection point had become a permanent resting place for a series of individual *poubelles* which were never retrieved, and more importantly, never cleaned. It had become a *poubelle* parking lot.

A *poubelle* parking lot is more than a casual collection of 12 - 15 garbage containers, it is also the depository zone for anything that does not fit into the containers, and anything that is left behind by the regional garbage collectors because it is in violation of environmental legislation. It is the informal repository for items which should be, but are not, taken by their owners to the local *déchètterie* / dump. Hence, it is a permanent small-scale dumping ground until the offending pile of refuse grows large enough and is finally noticed by the general maintenance crew of the village and carted off.

I reassured myself that soon we would be leaving this unsightly mess. And at our new home we had more distance between our front door and the neighborhood collection point, which was down the street and around the corner.

Directly across (about six feet) from our front door at rue Molière, was an irregular, triangular sliver of pavement approximately two feet deep at its base and tapering to a point where the narrow street made a slight bend. I had casually looked at this tiny plot of public pavement, thinking that someday I would put a planter box there, care for it, and grow a vine up the wall as a pleasant camouflage for an otherwise blank wall. (It seems, I have a genetic pre-disposition for looking at even the most mundane and functional of spaces with an eye to making them more attractive.)

One day, a mysterious yellow dot appeared; sprayed onto the pavement. What could it signify? I began to sleuth out the possibilities and found that there were similar yellow dots appearing in the neighborhood. Within a few days it became disappointingly clear. My heart sank as I saw the yellow dot replaced by the letters c-o-n-t-e-n-e-u-r-s. *Conteneurs*! This would be one of the new collection points for the garbage containers! Images of the *poubelle* parking lot sprung up before my eyes. Perhaps, you think that I am a pessimist, and that I should think lovely thoughts about the higher qualities of human nature. But my experience of *la vie en France*, as I had come to know it, alerted me to the inevitable. So, when the first errant *poubelle* attempted to take up residence across from our front door I decided to act.

Instinctively, I had saved the original pamphlets distributed by the regional organization responsible for this program. The pamphlet laid out the conditions and use of the new garbage containers. Little did I know how important extra copies of this pamphlet would be to keep the space in front of our home from becoming a *poubelle* parking lot. People with long established residences in the neighborhood followed the rules. But each time there was a new neighbor; there was a new test of the rules and personal tolerance.

The "dust-bin shuffle" continues even to this day when there is a changeover of residence, or at times of selective remembering, when people want to rid themselves of accumulated waste; at the time of birthday parties, carnival, summer fetes, and, of course, Christmas, New Years, and other holidays when waste seems to proliferate. It is one of those unpleasant constant reminders of incivility that haunts every day of life in France. In fairness I should say, it happens not every day, but it does happen every week - three times a week. Containers always seem to appear well in advance of the designated 8 pm guideline, the night before garbage pick-up. But there is a lapse, sometimes of days, before retrieval is made. One unexpected stroke of good fortune is that the *poubelles* come with the home address clearly labeled on the outside. After a reasonable period has elapsed, and all respectable containers have found their way home, the test begins.

Linda, in her optimism, considers that perhaps Madame or Monsieur might be ill, or perhaps away from home. Personally, it is a puzzle to me that such illnesses or absences only seem to impact the retrieval of the *poubelles*. All *poubelles* under a variety of imagined circumstances seem to find their way to the pickup point in time for collection. Illness seems only to strike when it comes time for retrieval. But I'll overlook this little peculiarity. Besides, for such rare occurrences as illness or absence, I am happy, as a good neighbor, to personally carry the *poubelle* to their door.

But I detect a pattern of behavior quickly. Seasoned, unfortunately, as I am to these behaviors, I first take to posting a copy of the "conditions of use" atop the offending garbage container with a big SVP and an arrow pointing to the time for placement and retrieval. When that does not make its point clear enough, or seems to be forgotten, I take the offending *poubelle* and place it near their front door, carefully placing it in a spot to cause some inconvenience, lest I be mistaken for their personal *poubelle* delivery service. The most persistent perpetrators of *poubelle* parking violations receive a personal appearance: "Rap Rap Rap" on their door. Intentionally, I do not wear a smile. I look surprised that I have found someone at home. The look is a cross between a Pink Panther pratfall and a dumb-as-a-fox detective -- a mix of Peter Sellers' Inspector Clouseau and Peter Faulk's Columbo. I say, "*Excusez-moi de vous déranger, je crois que ce poubelle appartient à vous Monsieur, Madame /* Excuse me for bothering you, I believe that this garbage container belongs to you", followed by a big "*Regardez, s'il vous plaît*", as I hand them their personal copy of the pamphlet. Fortunately, this last *pièce de résistance* has been necessary only once.

Remember the neighbors with the high-volume television? So far, they are the only people to make a challenge. They applied to the *Mairie / City Hall* for permission to place their garbage container in the exterior rather than interior to their home. There is such an exception to the rule when particularly small homes are occupied by many people. After proudly displaying their authorization to place their "*bac exterior*". I still had one more volley. I reminded them that the permission to place the garbage container on the exterior was exterior to THEIR house, not exterior to MY house. When faced with their own garbage container exterior to their own home, they soon applied for a smaller garbage container and found a place for it inside. *Voila!*

Remember, I am not talking about garbage here. I am talking of an environment created by people's behavior that colors everyday life. An everyday tension of incivility hangs in the air. It is exhausting. More importantly, it is demoralizing.

### An Update from France Spring

> Well folks, the **Big Move** has happened at last! During the Month of May we promised ourselves we would take the plunge and make the move from the little house at *09 Rue General Fraisse* (*Cœur de Village*) to *10 rue Molière* (*le petit jardin de l'âme*).

It has been two years, three months and 20+ days (but who's counting) since we arrived, and we finally were able to sleep in our bed in our own bedroom, eat dinner in our garden and swim in our pool! The lights work, the plumbing works, the kitchen works. We will have to wait until winter to see if the heat really works – but we are finished. Although we find occasional surprise "souvenirs", we have successfully removed any trace of the recalcitrant French workmen that once occupied this place. It looks remarkably like the home we envisioned 10 years ago. There is a long list of winter interior decoration projects developing. But at last, a gentle spirit enlivens these walls. After much sweeping and scrubbing and several trips to the local dump, we have been able to unwrap the remnants of a life we brought to France. This seems not so much like the finish, but rather the beginning of what we hoped for.

In the weeks prior to our move – so many of the people we see every day in the market asked us if we had moved. We finally began to tell them "Yes, indeed we have moved" because it became just too difficult to continue to tell them "*pas encore* / not yet". Our relocation did not actually involve the moving of any furniture since Cœur de Village will now be rented out as a furnished vacation house. However, one little vignette will give you a better idea how most locals make the move from one house to another.

As we made one of our frequent trips to collect clothes, and miscellaneous personal items from Cœur de Village, our neighbors were assembled in what we thought was the usual "*apéritifs a la rue*", when suddenly there appeared a three-cushioned antique leather sofa, its legs thrust out of the window on the *deuxième étage* / third floor, into the airspace above the street. I stopped loading the car to participate. Ruth Page could not have choreographed the event better: no ropes, no ladders, no pulleys. There were just sets of gaping hands flailing from the window above and those reaching from the street below with a prayer in between. Somehow, the descending sofa was met with grace, and quickly shuffled through the window at the ground floor of the house next door; presumably the new owners of "air sofa". This feat of *legerdemain* was accomplished amidst a surprise summer afternoon rain shower, which no one seemed to notice.

We are now in the process of settling in, creating shelving, and remembering where things are from day to day, until they find a permanent place in our new home. The pressure was on to make all look wonderful for the arrival of a small tour group from INTERNATIONAL LIVING. We hosted a reception for the group and Linda spent time touring the area with them and making connections with local realtors since the tour was for Americans interested in purchasing property in the south of France. We hope to entice a few B&B clients from the group as they plan their return visits to the area in search of just the right property.

The evening was a success and our guests were both suitably impressed, as well as pleasantly surprised, to see that someone has done what they hope to do. We ended the evening with a lovely dinner with our English-speaking friends whom we had invited to share their stories and their experiences of purchasing and building a life in the south of France.

Now, Linda is happily working away in the garage cutting and sanding rough wood planks into beautiful rustic shelves for our kitchen. When she is finished I will stain them and polish them with a wax finish, then she will put them up. We make a good team.

An update from France would not be complete without a recent scoop on "poodle poop". My comments over the past two years have come to the attention of the Maven of Etiquette, Ms. Manners, and I have discovered there is quite a following on this social phenomenon, especially among my readers in the USA. Ms. Manners is encouraged and reports that there have been signs of awareness here in

France that "Crotte is not Chic". Some nearby cities (Montpellier and Pézenas) have shown signs that they are ready to publicly expose poopers. Signs about fines and doggie litterbags have appeared in Pézenas. Some streets are noticeably cleaner. Nearby, Marseillan has published a campaign during the summer, which becomes effective in September to fine offending dog owners. Recent articles appeared along with posters : *Stop aux déchets canins! – C'est pas moi c'est mon chien – Pas de crotte de chiens dans nos rues !*

Alas, Florensac has not been so *"avant-garde"*, but I ask myself, can progress be far behind? Recently, our neighbors did acknowledge with appreciation that rue Molière has been cleaner since the Americans have taken an interest in keeping the street clean. And, do I dare say, that I have managed to shame two French residents not to use Rue Molière as a toilet for their dogs. One day as I gave an audible sigh, and retrieved the offending pile with a plastic bag. The doggie owner came over to me and said in French "I'll take care of it" – taking the bag from me to the trash bin. I was glad to know that guilt still works, even in France in the 21st century. For the moment, I have turned down an appointment from George Bush as "Quality of Life Attaché" in the newly liberated Iraq until we get this poop completely scooped here in France.

This Sunday we allowed ourselves a "play date" and will go to the Opera in Montpellier for the *Marriage of Figaro*. Later this week we have two sets of guests arriving. B&B reports in the area say that B&B business from the USA seems a little slow this year, and we can attest to that. After all, the dollar buys less this year in Europe than any year in recent history. But, I am happy to say that at last, *we* have arrived at le petit jardin de l'âme

**A basic law of physics: If it held wine, it will hold water**

The creation of our swimming pool spread over a lengthy period, with most of the work accomplished between the summer of 2001, ending, at last, beyond the scope of this book, in autumn of 2004. At least I hope the pool story is truly finished.

When we first purchased the property that would one day become le petit jardin de l'âme, there were three large reinforced concrete wine vats on the property. Their exact age was not known, but they were probably built sometime after World War II, perhaps as late as the 1950s. Two of the wine vats stood side by side. They were two stories tall, and built to hold about 100 cubic meters of wine each (that's more than 26 thousand gallons of wine in each vat). From the very first day we were told that these behemoths were impossible to convert to useable space, but we refused to believe it. Even in the most primitive state of the project, Linda and I envisioned using one of the vats as the supporting structure for a swimming pool. Inspired by a kind of reverse scripture analogy, we figured that if they held wine, they could hold water.

Our plan was met with disbelief, but the first masons on the project were happy to take our money and entertain the fantasies of the crazy Americans. For us, strangely enough, it was a practical matter. Either we must find a way to make these spaces useful or live with mountains of useless concrete and vacant space. The openings to the interior of these vats were small; one square wooden grate at the top of each approximately 18" x 18" for receiving grapes for fermentation, and one opening at the bottom large enough for a small child to crawl through when the time came to clean the vats.

First, we had to create a larger opening to the interior. Using an industrial strength diamond saw, the cement tops were cut open. Later, an archway was made at the bottom of one vat where a staircase would eventually be built in its interior. The second vat, the vat that stood next to our "some-day-it-will-be a terrace", was, to be our swimming pool. We both could "see" it clearly as a distant mirage, and went about our calculations, giving instructions for establishing the future depth of the pool and the level where it would meet the terrace. This, it must be said, was only a twinkle in our mind's eye at the time and beyond comprehension for the masons.

For several years the opened vats sat there, as workman after workman shook his head, grateful that we had not employed him to tackle the completion of this project.

Eventually, Linda calculated the interior space of one of the vats and created the plans for a staircase that would lead to our B&B rooms on the *premiere* and *deuxième étage* / second and third floors. This was a more gracious and practical entry to the rooms than the old entrance through the garage. It made good use of the interior vat space and preserved the structural supports to the "someday-it-will-be-a-swimming pool" in the vat next to it.

In the summer of 2001, as the rest of the renovation project advanced to a point where the terrace and the pool designs were to be joined, we enlisted the necessary structural engineer, and eventually searched for pool contractors. By this time, it took less imagination to envision where this pool would be built, next to our terrace, on the *deuxième étage* / third floor. But, it still required a bit of creative thinking as to how this would be accomplished. One pool contractor was simply not up to the creative design task. He liked to build conventional cement boxes placed safely in the ground. Another, had lots of flare, but had mistaken us for a member of the Forbes 500. And another, as if in a fairy tale, was just right. All had agreed that in this elevated position it was best to finish the pool with a vinyl liner, a product that I was skeptical about, but we decided to go with the unanimous choice of the experts on this one.

Before we proceed, let me try to assist you in imagining this pool. First, as I have mentioned, but have found often escapes being heard the first time around, it is UP. We walk into the pool from our terrace which is on the deuxième étage / third floor. There is a lovely view of rooftops and treetops, and we can see the mountains in the distance and the western setting sun. This elevated position makes it a bit unusual being in a village that dates, at least, from the 10th century. The size of the pool, as pools go, is small, a little more than 3x5 meters / approximately 10 x 17 feet. It is meant for our personal pleasure, for a leisurely cool-down, not an Olympic event. It is a private space for Linda and me. A water fountain, a cypress tree and a flowering vine separate this little haven from the nearest

B&B room. The pool was built using the existing walls of the old vat. A new reinforced floor was created to separate the bottom of the pool from the technical equipment, which is at ground level, inside the vat. Admittedly, it is an unusual use of an impossible space. You will not find this design in any do-it-yourself, quick, and easy pool kits available at your local hardware store. Now, with this picture developing in your mind, I will continue the story.

Work began in earnest the summer of 2002. Our mason (mason number three, now), in consultation with the pool-man, completed all the preliminary preparation of structure and surfaces. The pool-man was to fit the plumbing and the technical equipment, and install the liner. Initially the pool man was very attentive and offered some creative ideas; we were pleased. The pool, it seemed, would be one of the few projects to be accomplished without a hitch so the pool-man was on my short list of competent tradesmen.

My first clue to a problem was the fitting of the plumbing. Oh, it worked all right, but this was plumbing that was done by someone in a hurry. Not the precise angles and close fit to the wall that seemed the hallmark of a good plumber. This plumbing looked a bit like the bottom of bowl of spaghetti. My tentative attempts at asking for a bit more precision were shrugged off; clearly my job was to pay for the work, not to supervise it. Well, I told myself, it will be hidden in the machine room. Plumbing aesthetics aside, the rest did in fact seem to go like clockwork. The opening created for the skimmer was a little crooked, but I was told that would be corrected (it was not). The liner had a few wrinkles; those I was told would eventually disappear in a few weeks with water pressure and the warmth of the sun. The pool was finished, and we paid the pool man.

Shortly after swimming commenced, we noticed water dripping in the machine room below. There was, in fact, nothing in this machine room now to be damaged, but dripping water and dampness made any possible real use of this room for storage impossible. Our mason was a bit embarrassed at the sight of water since he had assured us that the walls and floor were watertight. More to the point, something was not right. We were able to swim in the pool. With that I was happy. But we had a problem. And thus, began a discussion that would continue for the next two years.

At first our complaints elicited surprise and an apparent quick fix, a minor adjustment here and there, we were told, would solve our problem. As the weeks passed without a remedy, the pool man's tone began to change. We were told we were unreasonable. "Of course, you will have water below, you have a pool above…", "You must have done something to cause this…", "You are splashing too much when you swim…".

The summer passed and in the spring, it was clear that we had a much bigger problem. Water was now a permanent cascade down the inside wall of the machine room. The wrinkles in the liner were more numerous, and in fact, the liner was pulling away from the walls of the pool. It seemed clear that there were significant amounts of water behind the liner. More of a concern to us was what we could not see. If the sides of the vat below were wet, how much water was trapped between the liner and the common wall between the pool and the wall of the house?

I began to take photos of the walls damp with water, of the wrinkles in the liner, and to document our attempts at correspondence.

The pool-man was becoming less responsive to telephone messages. But when I deposited my pictures in his letterbox, he came to see for himself; not to assess the problem, it turns out, but to accuse me of having caused the problem. The only explanation for the wrinkles in the liner, in his opinion, was that I must have emptied all the water out of the pool during the winter, therefore taking the pressure off the liner and allowing it to wrinkle. Aside from the fact that this was not true, it did not begin to address the flow of water we were experiencing in the machine room below.

By this time, my French was beginning to fail me. I had neither the technical "pool vocabulary" nor the debating skills to continue conversations in French with an uncooperative pool man. I enlisted the help of a couple of English speaking friends. They were qualified in many ways: first, they had a pool with a liner and had had some difficulties with their own installation years ago. Second, they were fluent in French, and had the kind of debating skills necessary to carry on a conversation with the pool-man. And most importantly, they were great client advocates! After one or two rounds with the pool man, we soon received the message that he was now in retirement, and we should contact his insurance company. Without the help of our friends I would not have known to ask for important documentation regarding his insurance coverage at the time of the installation of the pool. This turned out to be crucial. That "sense of being in hurry" that I first witnessed was beginning to become clear to me. The installation of our pool was to be a quick and easy job, just before the pool man closed shop. He did not want to hear from us. And so, a new pool-chapter; how to deal with the insurance company, opened before us.

Personally, I was expecting the worst from the insurance company. In this case, I am happy to say, I was wrong. The claims persons came to the site, quickly agreed that something was wrong, and asked only for some tests to determine the extent of the problem. We spent the summer of 2003 documenting and testing. When was the problem worse? When, if ever, did it stop? Was it a problem with the plumbing or a problem with the liner? I am good at this kind of detective work, so it does not bother me if I know we are working together. And at last, we were.

Over the summer there was one expert sent from the insurance company who would have us cut through the bottom of the pool to diagnose the problem. Aside from costs and the structural impact of opening the reinforced concrete bottom of the pool, everyone agreed that perhaps we could approach this in a less drastic manner. A second expert was called. His contribution was to tell us of a testing mechanism that could be employed, but he himself did not have the abilities to do this test. In December of 2003, a third expert was called, who performed the test and concluded that there were three leaks, all in the liner itself. In his opinion, given the history of the problem as we described it, they had probably existed from the very first day.

We agreed that no one was likely to use the pool in December, even in the south of France, so a plan was made to make a temporary repair in May of 2004, and to see if in fact, that solved the problem. At last we were on to something, and we were working cooperatively with someone. This last pool expert also recommended that an emergency overflow drain be installed. An emergency overflow drain was simply a hole drilled into the cement bottom, so that any possible water from condensation or overflow would have an easy escape and be directed to a pre-determined spot. Technically, this should have been included in the original plans, but it was the leaks in the original liner that were our primary problem. The temporary repair was made, and an emergency overflow drain was created. *Voila*, problem solved. Plans were made to install a new liner in September after the 2004 swim season. We took the opportunity to upgrade the liner.

After a series of events like this, I am faced with some internal conflicts. On one hand, I am grateful for the resolution. And I am pleased to have found a reliable pool company for continued service. On the other hand, I have spent a good deal of two years of my life, my time and the time of good friends, to document a problem of incompetence and fraud by the original workman. This story, on this specific project, as you well know by now, is a story like many that have been repeated many times during our life in France. I have learned over time, to become more alert to the potential of incompetent workmen, but deceit is what it is: difficult to detect until after one has been duped.

Our swimming pool, modest in size, big in impact, is a joy to me. And on a hot summer's day I can jump in and cool down two or three or more times a day. A late-night dip in the summer moonlight is a wonderful nightcap. But, I wonder, how much do I need to swim to wash away the bad feelings that came with it.

*Even the victorious, carry with them battle scars*
-The Author

During this time, I write in the journal:

July 2003

When I search for signs of improvement. I see some benefits of medication. I can sleep most nights, and while fueled with a full tank of Prozac, I am more able to address some of the day-to-day incivilities of life in France. I am, in general, less anxious about expressing myself more clearly and directly in response to my anger and irritation. But I also ask myself, is this the environment in which I want to continue to live?

We have successfully completed -- as much as any old house is ever completed – our renovation project. It is a lovely place. I believe that, in general, we have even created the ambiance we intended. But we are no longer together, except that we live in this same space. We are no longer of the same spirit as we once were. This is a deep sadness for me. On top of the generalized depression about discovering the shadow side of everyday life in France, I am very sad at the loss of our closeness as a couple.

Even though surrounded by the externals of *la vie en france,* the reality of life in France is far from our once upon a time dream. Within our garden, protected by stone walls, life is very close to what I hoped for. But, it is an uneasy existence because so much energy is diverted to defenses and protection of our space from intrusion. In a paradoxical way, it is like having an elephant in the living room - always present. Even as I try wearing blinders to ignore these irritations, they are "present" because of the energy I use to avoid them. And, then of course, there are the unmistakable intrusions, like when I step in a pile of crotte and accidentally drag it into the house on my shoes, or the necessary crotte surveillance, removal and street washing before guests arrive. I had hoped for a life integrated and supported by our surroundings, instead, I find myself on constant alert to defend against the inconsiderate habits that surround us.

My thoughts of suicide have receded somewhat. No longer is it a daily battle. But once having crossed the threshold of suicide as a possibility, it no longer seems a desperate move but simply one way to end the intolerable: not immediate, and not in desperation, but a considered choice which essentially says I am truly, truly tired. I want to stop. I give up.

There are brief moments when I catch myself – almost by surprise – thinking, "I'm going to make this work!" Our home is lovely, despite the French workmen, not, as I had hoped, because of fine old-world craftsmanship.

Our life here – or rather my life – could be lived largely behind our walls and in our courtyard and terrace, with tolerable time-limited moments of interactions with the locals for the necessities. I am happy with the home we have created and search for signs that within these walls where we might again be the couple we once were with a shared dream. I think that I could enjoy our life with just the two of us and some friends on occasion. I did not intend to live my life on an island. But, when I try to envision how to make this life in France work, that is the image I see. Currently our vision of life is not a shared vision. We seem to have gravitated to opposite ends of the color spectrum. We look at the way of life in France and I see black, you see white.

On this 14 July celebration here, I am sitting on our beautiful terrace. I have just finished a swim in the pool to cool down. From our terrace, I can see most of the fireworks because they clear the rooftops. I am here above, while you, my love, have chosen to go down to the street near the park among the crowd. This perhaps is the symbol of our life in France. France is more enjoyable for me, at a distance. You like being among the people. Once, I thought I would like that also, and hoped for that. But now, you are there, and I am here. Most importantly, we are not together. The *Fête Nationale* of France, 14 July, is a symbol of what our life is like in France. French *Liberté* divides us.

## A Change of Focus

The change of focus that accompanied the move to le petit jardin de l'âme was the focus on the arrival of guests. This was a pleasant change and one for which we had been preparing since our arrival in France. On many practical matters, we had the benefit of our previous Bed & Breakfast experience in Chicago from which to draw. And, at last, we experienced the enjoyment that comes from the realization of doing what we came to France to do. We looked forward to being B&B hosts. We fully expected that during our first years, the number of guests would be few and that leisurely pace suited us perfectly. Our B&B clients came largely from past B&B guests who had stayed in our restored Victorian home in Chicago, and from an assortment of colleagues and clients from our past professional lives.

Seeing life in France through the eyes of our guests was, in many ways, a relief to the way of life that we had so far experienced. And we enjoyed providing the romance of the south France that our guests had come to experience. We encouraged guests to bicycle through the vine-covered French countryside, prepare a picnic lunch by shopping at the local vegetable market, and purchase good tasting wine at amazingly low prices; all part of *la vie en France* that makes France one of the most visited countries in the world. Perhaps, I wondered, France is best seen through the rose-colored lens of vacation.

For our B&B guests, Linda was the best "up front person", making most of the contact with guests, answering questions and setting up breakfast in the courtyard or dining room. I chose to do the computer work, create brochures, print guest information, liaison with the tourist office, and prepare the occasional apéritives and *Table d'Hôtes*. I conscientiously avoided conversations that might inevitably include questions such as "How do you like life in France". When this was unavoidable, it was important to keep comments brief and refocus on our guests' enjoyment. Creating the ambiance of the France we wanted to share also helped refocus our own lens for a while.

Entertaining B&B guests or personal friends during this first summer in our new home involved learning how to use the wonderful new kitchen we had created, experimenting with meals on the great stone barbeque in our courtyard, and using the antique brasserie rotisserie we had purchased years ago. We now had a growing number of English friends and enjoyed entertaining and being entertained by them. Because of her daily walks, Linda was often the happy recipient of gifts of seasonal fruits and vegetables from the gardens of kindly elderly neighbors: figs in fig season, cherries in abundance, pumpkin-like *courgettes* in autumn, olives after curing several months, and a steady flow of freshly made *oriellettes*. These were reminders of the gentle people and the sunnier side of life in France that we had hoped to find.

In our garden, there was much yet to learn about plants and planting in this Mediterranean climate, and our own specific adaptations for light and shade in our courtyard. Our garden, like our pool and our home itself is comfortable but modest in size. However, its impact is large. *Le petit jardin* was becoming just what we had hoped it would be. It was the centerpiece of our summer entertaining. And symbolically, it was that little place where we could offer a special brand of tranquil refreshment for the soul, to nourish our guests. And for us, perhaps, a place to recover the life we had dreamed of. It was, what we had envisioned, a le petit jardin de l'âme.

### An Update from France – Autumn

> As I write this update, it is a "Masterpiece Theatre" kind of evening. I feel a bit like Alistair Cooke; wearing my cardigan, sitting by the fire, a glass of sherry on the table. Although we have lived our life without television for more than two years, I expect to hear, any moment now, that familiar *rondeau*, trumpet fanfare from *Jean-Joseph Mouret* that introduced those BBC/PBS programs on Sunday evening.

No, we have not moved to England. We are very much in the south of France. However, our autumn nights have become cool enough to warrant a fire in the fireplace. The days are bright but crisp. That long hot summer is only a memory. This year's *vendange* was early. The dry summer made the harvest ready in late August. Everyone predicts there will be a small harvest, but a good year for wine. (Translate that – more expensive). An early harvest means there is a longer lazy autumn season now between the end of the harvest and the winter's cold. It is my favorite time of the year.

Linda fulfilled one of her French fantasies this year by helping one of the families in the village during the harvest. There she was shoulder-to-shoulder, bucket to bucket clipping the grapes by hand, as many still do in the area. She was delighted. Me, I prefer drinking more than picking the fruit of the vine!

Some afternoons are still warm enough to eat lunch in our garden. It is like an extra room where we live. A couple of birds have taken up residence in the garden rafters somewhere. They have now come to expect that I shake our breakfast breadcrumbs from the tablecloth onto the garden floor. Although most of our garden is trimmed back ready for its winter rest, I have delayed trimming the solanum because its blue flowers still form a lovely cascade from the beam of the old roof in the corner of the courtyard. The other day we noticed that we were not the only ones thinking about the coming winter. Some bees were busy buzzing about – well, "busy as bees" you might say. Our lunchtime entertainment included watching them closely. It seemed to me that at least one couple had given up the drudgery of pollen collection for some sweeter activities. I think they were practicing their "snuggle-up" positions for the coming winter. I found myself quietly humming Cole Porter's little tune ♪ "Birds do it, bees do it, … Let's Fall in Love ♪. We shared a giggle and realized how our lives have changed.

Speaking of the facts of life, we were honored in September to be invited to the birthday celebration of Louis, our good friend. Also known as Monsieur "Good Morning" and "Louis XIV" in some of my earlier Updates, Louis was celebrating his 92nd Birthday. Indeed, just getting up in the morning is a celebration at his age! Nevertheless, he invited us to share the day with his family. It was an entire French afternoon since we were the only "non-family" invited. The range of ages went from 92 years old (Louis himself) to the most recent baby, two months old, and 24 family members in-between. Near the end of the afternoon, the conversation turned to opera and Louis treated us to one of his favorite arias. The room gradually came to silence as he sang. Amazing!

Much of our time is spent on putting the final touches on our house. I expect that could go on ...f-o-r-e-v-e-r. However, we can enjoy our home and live as we hoped to live. Recently, I have been on a "faux finishing frenzy". Our walls in the master bathroom are now wonderfully compatible with our tiles. Real light fixtures are up, and we are ready for hanging pictures. I am pleased with my faux marbling on our fireplace in the master bedroom. The original fireplace façade is black marble, but the chimney and sides were broken up plaster. It is now very difficult to tell which is faux and which is fine marble. Linda recently transformed a *port-manteau* / hall tree, from a garage sale reject to a House & Garden Treasure. I added some faux finishes, and a blue bird for extra "wow value" and now our guests ask us where we found such a lovely piece. Just another "silk purse from a sow's ear"

We are pleased with the "word of mouth" referrals we receive from our B&B guests. Moreover, it pleases us to watch our guests and personal friends examine our home with childlike curiosity. Recently, during an evening with friends, Linda, returned to the dining room, after a change of dinner place settings. Our friends, chagrinned, confessed that they had been examining some of the silverware during our absence. Others admire the wood ceilings and the stone arch. "Sorry", they say. "I can't stop staring". It is a joy for us, and for them. It is part of the magic of le petit jardin de l'âme

It is true, France was beginning to look and feel like home. More than a physical place to "hang our hat", an important part of being "at home" was the development of friendships. And while the number of brief, social encounters with French people grew, our friendships were made among the English-speaking people who had, like us, come to live in France. These friendships made during these three years among the English-speaking community proved to be a source of welcome comfort and mutual enjoyment.

During our first year in France we had focused our attention on efforts of integration into the French speaking community, perhaps to the exclusion of potential friendships among the growing number of English who settled here. But as time passed, and frustrations with French language, French workmen, and French behavior grew, we discovered that we were probably being too hard on ourselves, and thereafter we let ourselves develop the friendships that came naturally – and most enjoyably. Many in this English-speaking community have fully integrated into a bilingual social life, having French friends and English friends. Among this group there are those who have discovered that their attempts to mix the two are generally not successful social occasions. Ironically, they observe, that it is the French who are stiff in these mixed social situations. Some of our English friends clearly prefer to live in France, but have limited contact with the French. It was good for us to see the range of possibilities and to set social expectations that worked for ourselves.

Now, freed from the experiences of renovation, we continued to hope that the life we came to live in France would gradually develop. We continued to take language courses, read the local newspapers, and make attempts at more extended conversations. But the ability to have a truly fluid conversation in French seemed forever impossible. We gradually came to realize that social occasions in the French language were stressful both for ourselves and for those French acquaintances with whom we made the effort. Our most enjoyable conversations -- free flowing, with feeling, nuance, and humor -- were in English and with English friends. I welcomed the lively repartee and intellectual stimulation. It was with these English friends that we began to develop an "adopted family" in France.

As we began to settle into a semblance of normal life at *le petit jardin,* the undercurrent of tension from our first three years continued to hang over us. The life in France that we had experienced so far, hovered like a shadow. Even as we tried to grow beyond those experiences, we continued to accentuate the positive, focus on our accomplishments thus far, and hope that the "and they lived happily ever after" chapter would be written soon.

*Le petit jardin de l'âme*

**Christmas 2003**

> There is no snow, except what we can see in the distance on the mountaintops. Our daytime temperatures are sunny, in the mid 50's Fahrenheit. And, at last, in our 3rd December here in France, even I can say we have created our home in France and Christmas has come. Of course, Linda "arrived" at this point much sooner than I, but ♪ It's Beginning to Look a Lot Like Christmas ♪.
>
> There are moments when I just sit by the fire and stare incredulously at our tree decorated under the big stone arch. Our trumpeting angels sit in grand style on the fireplace mantle and our Christmas crèche is near the stairway. Florensac streets cannot compare with the grandeur of Chicago's Magnificent Mile. Nevertheless, there is a more festive aire in the village this year. Each year we see more lighted balconies, and this year, the shops in the plaza have several Christmas trees decorated at their storefronts. "The Christmas Rush" in France is most likely to be at the food counters for chestnuts, oysters, coquilles Saint Jacques and Bûche Noël. Just the other day I was nearly trampled in the market. I had mistakenly placed myself in a precarious position -- between the crowd and the foie-gras-lady giving free samples!

We have several milestones to celebrate this year. This is the year when...

- We made the big move from our temporary house (at *Cœur de Village*) to the house we purchased over ten years ago at *petit jardin de l'âme*. At last it is HOME.
- We unpacked the last of our 292 boxes from the big Chicago move in 2001. Most things are now placed where we can find them and not buried under a pile construction debris. Our silver, glass, and dinnerware were like lost treasures found, now to be enjoyed by new friends. Our artwork seems made to hang on these walls -- remnants of a past life made new.
- Our wardrobe boxes are unpacked. We now dress as civilized human beings, rather than wearing recycled t- shirts and patched jeans. Linda is a lovely sight in casual skirts and dresses. I am sorry to say that some of my clothes must have shrunk a little while in storage!
- Cleaning the living room means using the "Hoover", as our English friends would say, and a feather duster, not a shovel and dump truck. It is amazing the effect that ridding ourselves of tons of construction debris has on my psyche.
- We have not seen a French plumber, electrician, mason, etc., for several months. "Renovation professionals" are history. We now have the ironic pleasure of hearing other peoples "Horror Stories" and feel relieved. That chapter is past.

> Our surprise this year was that we became experienced in using the French Medical Care System. Linda was hospitalized in January, August, November, and December. Now all is fine. I must say that the results of our enforced research resulted in an A+ rating for medical care in France. I am sure you know that an A+ rating from me is hard to come by. Thankfully, we discovered that French doctors, nurses etc are much better than French plumbers, electricians, and masons.
>
> Our French is improving, each of us in our own way. Linda is now receiving complements from the local Florensacois on her French. Perhaps this is a secondary benefit of conversations with doctors and nurses regarding atrial flutter and atrial fibrillation, or her daily morning

trips to the market for breakfast pastries. I have moved on in a different way – for better or worse. I no longer care if I am "getting it right", I now say it the best I can and am interested in "getting my point across". There are times when I have found that my past attempts have been just too tentative, and perhaps, too focused on correctness for the French to hear what I mean.

The tradesman working on the house down the street got my point. He no longer lets his German Shepherd poop in front of our house! After a few briefs, civil but direct, interrogatory sentences in French, about the offending pile in front of my house, I do not know if I said "Cochon / Pig!", which is what I meant, or did I say "couchons / let us lay down"? Nevertheless, there are no more poops from his pooch on rue Molière. Sorry, I just get so excited about this nasty French habit. And on another day, at the crowded market in Pézenas, some woman decided to stand in a recently vacated parking space. I waited a moment for her to move as I made my parking intentions known, only to discover that she was standing there, saving the space with a body block, until her friend, not yet visible, returned with the car. Although I lost the verbal wrestling match, over what seemed at the time to be the last available parking space on the planet, it felt good to stand up for myself in French at this "shout-out at the OK Corral".

I might elaborate on Julius Caesar's famous description of Gaul in the first century: Gaul is divided in to three parts; *the good, the bad and the ugly*.

On a more civilized note, we have arrived at a time in our life in France where we are able to enjoy visiting a fine local domaine for an afternoon book launch and wine tasting. The book, written by the son of some friends, focuses on the Languedoc and inspires us to write our own. More and more, we are finding and enjoying some of the hidden treasures of France off the beaten path.

We now celebrate a regular Home Eucharist on the third Sunday of each the month. Twelve to fifteen people attend. And, we celebrated our 2nd Annual English Lessons and Carols with 150 attending at the church in nearby Fontès. We enjoy a growing familiarity with our new home and neighbors. Monsieur "Good Morning' – age 92 -- like a *Petit Père Noël* -- brings us fresh Oriellettes from his own kitchen. We, in turn, bring him fresh roasted chestnuts from the market square. Our neighbors on rue Molière feel free to step right into our living room as they bring news of the day or to make an inquiry. After all, they saw our shutters closed, when they should be open; or opened when they are usually closed, was everything all right? In addition, we now receive "billets doux" slipped through the mail slot to wish us "Bon Fête", "Joyeux Noël".

In the New Year we will take a few days in Paris to celebrate a belated 25th Wedding Anniversary (December 02). We also will renew a New Year's Tradition that had gotten away from us since our move to France. We take some time in the New Year to reflect and to set our personal and joint goals. This practice helped us to be where we are today.

I am not at all sorry to end the "This Old House" chapter of our life in France. On the spring horizon, there are flowers to be planted, lunches in the garden, bicycling in the countryside, wines to be tasted, friends to enjoy, and a big prayer of thanksgiving that we survived the adventure to le petit jardin de l'âme.

*Life may not be the party we had hoped for, but we might as well dance while we're here.*
-Unknown, attributed to Ellie Nemeth

# Epilogue

## Of Endings, Beginnings, and Endings

Every book needs to end somewhere, and so it is that I choose to end this book with our Christmas letter of 2003. Our adjustment to life in France has continued some years beyond that date, and in fact the "and they lived happily ever after" chapters are still waiting to be written. As I write this Epilogue, it is now more than five years since we first moved to France and there are many more stories to tell about *la vie en France*. For me, life in France is much like a trompe d'œil tableau, not always what it seems.

Typically books of this genre have a predictable happy ending. All the dust, dirt, debris are cleared away, faux pas are fitted with forgiveness. Heartache, anxieties, and things that go bump in the night are given a positive framing under a bright southern sun and azure sky. But from the beginning, this candid reflection on the glorious and gruesome realities of creating a new life in France was to go beyond *"la vie en rose"*, to explore both the brilliance and the shadow side of life in the Midi. And so, such fairy tale endings are left to authors and titles in the New Fiction or Romance sections of the bookshelf. After five years I can say we have only begun, and the journey continues in this land of  *A Bright Sun & Long Shadows*

We are thankful to have survived the journey to *le petit jardin*. I had hoped we might have thrived on our new life in France. That is not the case. We are changed, of that I am sure, and it is clear to us and to the local French that we have made a significant investment and plan to stay. Now, Linda and I have different reasons for arriving at this same conclusion. It remains to be seen whether these challenges have brought out the best in us. Are we made better persons for having lived the experience? Or has this simply been a very expensive and painful lesson in French?

In some ways, my experience of life in France has heightened my awareness that, in retrospect, I lived a privileged life, not necessarily in the material sense of immense wealth, though we were, and are, comfortable, but in the sense of living my life with the confidence that comes when one knows the language and can use it to convey nuance and complexity; the advantages that come with a good education and knowledge of local custom, and the power one has when identified with a perceived majority - in this case, white Anglo-Saxon male. I expected change and challenge in our new life in France. What I did not expect was that in this new land, I would be meeting these challenges from the disadvantaged position of a minority. No matter how proficient my French, it is unlikely that I would be mistaken for a Frenchman. And, I do not wish to become French, even if it were possible. I had underestimated the impact of being forever an outsider. The challenge to build a new life in this new land is the challenge to build a new life from the position of a minority.

Both Linda and I have had the occasional experience of being described by those in the village as "Florensacois", a real member of the village. It is a complement that we willingly accept, but we know in our hearts that it is not so. Will it ever be so?

I sometimes think of a sequel to *A Bright Sun & Long Shadows*. A sequel might address still more stories of adjustment to French life, post-construction at le petit jardin de l'âme. It would include the progressive adaptation to the undercurrent of tensions of *la vie en France* that come from outside, and the effect the tensions from our different and polarized views of la *vie en france* has had on our marriage. It would follow the ups and downs of depression through to its conclusion. It would include the joys of the development of important friendships, and more word-pictures of what our cross-cultural life has become after more than five years investment of personal and financial capital. And, it would include a touch of fancy in the tales of our furry French friend Bijou Bunné. But for now, the story must end.

As we end these chapters, I remember another, long ago ending and beginning from our life of "once upon a time".

We are not new to life changes. Many years ago, Linda and I each left our separate, established lives and careers, to make, what at the time, was a controversial life change. We moved to Chicago to grow a new life together. Twenty-five years later we were able to say that it had been hard work and a wonderful life. In our letter of Christmas 2000, which you read in the opening pages, we envisioned what life might be like as we struck out again to make a new life in a new land.

> The name of our new home – le petit jardin de l'âme -- says something about our approach to life in general. It is good for the soul that we be uprooted now and again…transplanted, trimmed, and pruned…

Now we're ready for the next great adventure in little garden of the soul.

At this point, as we grow our lives in the land of France's Midi, I am only able to say that the adventure has been, well, much more than expected. It remains to be seen if we can truly grow where we have planted ourselves. And it remains to be seen what manner of garden might grow in a land where there is such *A Bright Sun & Long Shadows*.

> *I love the light for it shows me the way. Yet the darkness shows me the stars.*
> -Og Mandino

# Appendix

## Living with daily deceptions

As I begin this section, I want to put the comments that follow in a proper context. One of the most difficult aspects of adjustment to life in France was an adjustment to a norm of everyday deceptions. I hope that I can adequately convey that this is not a moral judgment. I have spent much too much time searching my personal, spiritual, religious, and psychological archeology for ruins and artifacts that might be the source of some unconscious neurotic reaction, judgmental attitude, or a position of moral superiority. And, although no one ever completely liberates themselves from that initial imprint of values passed on to us in childhood, most of us, in maturity, are able to moderate and modulate those original indelible marks of good old Roman Catholic guilt (or Jewish guilt, or Calvinism, or Puritanism, or … fill in the blank with your own special brand). In fact, in our adult lives most people realize that there is some pragmatic sensibility for having congruence in what we believe and say and do. Although some of our pragmatic adaptations of truth telling may be more clever, some straight forward, some more creative, eventually we find a place of equilibrium where what we say reflects what we believe and do, or intend to do when communicating with others. It has been my experience of life in France that many people live lives in a perpetual exercise of cognitive dissonance. What is said and done may bear little or no resemblance one to the other. It seems perfectly natural in France to live incongruously.

Early in our preparations for life in France we read with interest the advice of some rather well-known cross-culture gurus. Experts advised a polite verbal formula with which to begin any and every request for help. A point well taken. Then, one expert continued, add a touch of creativity. The French love theater, so give them theater. As it turns out, this touch of creativity need not have anything to do with the truth of the matter. It is intended to get the other person's attention, to come to your aide. This deception has been habitualized into a cultural norm. Making up a story to persuade someone to do something that you would like done is normal. Little did I understand at the time that replacing factual communication with a sense of dramatic fiction was but the tip of a cultural iceberg.

For the sake of making some semblance of order out of a rather freewheeling way of life, I have grouped experiences of every day deception into three areas: Trickery, The Diplomacy of Denial, and The Way of the Paysan.

Trickery, living by your wits, is a prized personal commodity in France. In spite of a long cultural heritage of Roman Catholicism, the French seem to have skipped the chapter on guilt. The Golden Rule seems also to have suffered something in translation. It is difficult to find an altruistic interpretation. In the French version of "Do unto others as you would have done unto you", a pragmatic adaptation in the form of "One hand washes the other" seems more to the point. In my continued efforts to understand puzzling behavior in which I often found myself holding the short end of the stick, I found Robert Darnton's book, THE GREAT CAT MASSACRE, and other episodes in French cultural history, helpful. Darnton, points out that our assumed familiarity with Mother Goose fairy tales, many based on Perrault's CONTES DE MA MÈRE L'OYE, often results in a failure to notice significant cultural differences in the French version of these stories which have been adapted as they crossed cultures. In examining French versions of these peasant tales, he explores the role of trickery as a survival skill, unusual ways of seeking one's fortune in a world of "dupe or be duped", and a folklore that demonstrates the folly of expecting anything more than cruelty from a cruel social order. With this as cultural background, I began to understand some of my experience in France in a new light. I still did not like being at the short end of the stick, but I now knew why this was inevitable. I was centuries behind, and way out of my league in developing this skill.

Many of our experiences of life in France, especially with tradesmen during our renovation project are not so far removed from the more primitive tales of Mother Goose. I need not repeat our tales from the first three years in France, but I merely mention here that I did not tell them all in the preceding chapters. There are more. Outwitting a stranger, a foe, or anyone perceived as authority or those perceived as having a fine fortune to be plundered is a way of life that remains alive and well. Contemporary versions of these tales are created each day.

Fortunately, Linda and I have outlived the initial trickery and libelous reports we feared and now have broadened our social network. After five years we have found a peer group. And have, in time, established our own personal history of integrity in a new land. Occasionally, we come up against the legendary discrepancies between what is said or written in matters of public policy or law that may bear little resemblance to what happens. And, as we become more familiar with laws in France, and our conversations with others focus on involvement in our respective communities, we are also more aware that circumventing the law is an everyday game played by all. However, this should not imply that it makes life fun. It is remnant of a way of survival where the *"joie de vivre"* for one comes at the other's expense. It fosters a worldview of winners and losers rather than a commitment to mutual success. In everyday parlance these discrepancies seem to be dismissed by a simple *"pas grave* / Oh it's not serious" or the proverbial "provençal shrug". There is no error admitted, not a tinge of guilt, remorse, or a sense of making amends. If someone is unfortunate enough to be caught, the French demonstrate their love of theatrics. Occasionally, our personal preference for having all our tax and personal accounting facts accurately reflect the way things are is received by some *fonctionnaires* as puzzling, and causes us, perhaps, an unnecessary expense. But we are still not comfortable with all that *la vie en france* has to offer.

The Diplomacy of Denial bears little resemblance to the faded glory of French as the language of diplomacy, when everyday life is lived with a daily dose of deception. Diplomatic Denial allows the person who is employing it to believe he has complied with your wishes while in fact doing nothing of the kind. Even when one has reached an (apparent) agreement on a task, the outcome or implementation may bear little resemblance to the plan. I have used the term Diplomatic Denial here not with a sense of morality, but rather in the sense of a coping mechanism. It is a temporary adjustment to allow everyone involved the time needed to experience the full impact of the situation. However, denial can be "catchy" and whole families, villages, and societies can share in the delay of facing a reality, making denial a way of life. To help clarify this point, here are yet a few, yet untold tales, to give you the Reader's Digest version of how diplomatic denial is used every day.

Early during our renovation project, in fact long before we moved to France, it became clear that directions for the work to be done, products to be purchased, and what the price included needed to be very specific. We are good at this sort of detail and organization. Plans were drawn to scale, photos were provided, and for more complex work, the photos were overlaid with sketches. But soon we discovered that the clearer we became, the more difficulty we had in making the finished job match the original specifications. In good humor, we joked that we would someday have to purchase another house just to use up the accumulated errors in tile purchases, bathroom fixtures etc. In fact, when we did purchase *Cœur de Village* we were able to re-use many of the "mistakes" from the original plans intended for *le petit jardin*.

In the first bathrooms to be completed we specified and discussed exhaust and ventilation. Linda was already familiar with a substandard practice where bathroom exhaust was vented into the space between the inner wall and the outside wall and we wished to avoid this. We clearly indicated that the ventilation was to go through the wall and to the outside, not simply up to the outside wall. We later discovered that while the ventilation appeared to have been put in place, in fact, it had not been ventilated to the outside. The humidity for the bath was ventilating into the space between the interior and exterior wall. In another situation, in conformity with requirements for ventilation for certain gas burning fireplaces, holes of 8-10 cm diameter needed to be cut through the thick, stone walls to the outside. Ignoring our red X's that marked the location for these holes, our plumber began to drill the holes where he could conveniently reach them rather than where we had placed the mark. On another occasion, Linda discovered that a wall, created to provide storage space in our home office, had managed to be misplaced even after she had precisely drawn the lines for the finished wall on the floor of the room. In these situations, as well as those in the preceding chapters, we had stopped expecting an admission of error. But we were not prepared for the workmen's assertion that they were doing what we had asked them to do. Yes, put in the ventilation fans, drill the holes, and put up the wall – but put them in the place marked on the plan. I'll spare you the numerous times we went through this exercise with the electrician. But imagine the potential for having this as a diplomatic mission with the placement of each electrical outlet! One workman who normally did good work was asked to complete his job by properly caulking around the new port-fenêtres that he installed. Clearly, he felt that finishing the installation by sealing around the windows was a job for someone else. He was not thrilled. But he did the job quickly. With a smile on his face and the typical exclamation, "Voila, jolie!" he showed Linda that he had now done what he had been asked to do. The job was not "jolie" at all. His beautiful, custom-made fine wood French doors had been installed with all the finesse of a five-year-old gone wild with a glue gun on his school art project

As time passed we learned of the importance for the French to "save face" in these situations. We no longer asserted that an error had been made since that seemed unacceptable. We simply insisted that we wished the project to be completed in the following manner, and repeated our original requirements. Workmen seemed to view this review of the plan as if it were a new development they were looking at for the first time. Acknowledgement often with a phrase "C'est *noté* / It is noted." Joining them in their denial seemed the diplomatic thing to do. In this process, based on mumbles and other more audible and visual responses from the workmen, we risked being mistakenly identified as overly demanding, and fickle people who often changed their mind or did not know what they wanted in the first place. Clearly, the face that is saved in "Saving Face" is a French face.

*Sixty Million Frenchmen Can't Be Wrong (Why We Love France But Not the French)*, is the title of a book by French/English Canadian journalists Jean-Benoît Nadeau and Julie Barlow. Chapters seven and eight were especially helpful to me in seeing this Diplomatic Denial (my term not theirs) on a grand scale. These chapters illustrate that the French national psyche has yet to deal with denial in two significant areas of their history; World War II, the unforgotten war, and Algeria, the unacknowledged war. In these critical moments of 20th century history, denial is at work on a national scale. To be fair, France is not alone in the use of this form of corporate denial. And our experience in village life is a rather small horizon by comparison. But the experience of Diplomatic Denial in everyday ways, has a personal and emotional cost, on both the large and small horizons of life that eventually cannot be denied.

By far, the most sinister of the everyday deceptions is The Way of The Paysan (The Ways of The Peasants). It is most sinister not in some criminal sense, although in some cases the law is broken; it is sinister in the way it silently creeps into everyday life and, often too late, you discover that it has encroached on your life. The forms of Trickery and Diplomatic Denial are as bright as daylight in comparison to The Way of The Paysan.

The Way of The Paysan is a phrase that I acquired because of a recurring theme in conversations where people, some new, and some who have lived here many years, would relate a personal experience about how they had discovered that there had been an infringement on their land or property rights over a period. Sometimes through astute detective work they were able to recover what had been lost, and, sometimes they discovered that because of the passage of time without a protest they had forfeited their right. One woman won back her legal right to reclaim her privacy. Neighbors had illegally created a window opening that overlooked her private living space. However, while having success in this matter, she is still trying to solve the mystery of large flying stones that enter her garage making dents in the hood of her automobile. We have also heard this story from a different angle (different window, different private space, different people). In this case the story tellers were the ones who created an opening and placed a window, knowing full well that what they were doing was illegal, but at the same time, placing the burden on their neighbor to make the complaint and follow through. This couple, it should be said, were not French but they give a good illustration of the effect of deception on the way of life; it is contagious. Incongruously, as they told us this story, it was clear they were proud of how clever they were to use this practice to their advantage. Another couple noticed that one year their neighbor's vineyard was expanding. A new line of vines had been planted suspiciously close to their property line. When a second line of new vines appeared, they decided that it was time to invest in a new official survey. They were very diplomatic, and of course, the *vigneron* demonstrated his surprise. But row-by-row they were in danger of losing their property to the ways of the *paysan*. We too, had an experience with these creeping ways. However, for us, at that time, we were not sufficiently wise to what was happening. We found ourselves later engaged in diplomatic negotiations with our neighbors, sensitively trying to resolve a matter that was, originally, an illegal intrusion into our space.

With this as background you can see that the anecdote "Doin' The Dustbin Shuffle" tells the same tale. In a rather mundane way it has that same *paysan* flavor. Clearly, I would prefer that the collection point for the garbage containers were elsewhere. But its location is a minor nuisance and minimal annoyance, if the rules are followed. The dustbin shuffle is a constant exercise in setting boundaries in a land where inch-by-inch one person's space is enhanced to the detriment of another. I would not be so certain of this inevitability if it had not happened at *Cœur de Village* and at other collection points in the village where there is less vigilance. The way of the paysan would, little-by-little, have the space in front of our home looking like the city dump.

By extension, the story of my late-night *tête a tête* with the neighbors as recounted in "An Acquired Taste" reflects this same battle with the creeping ways of the paysan. I am thankful that, in general, the volume on their television can no longer be heard from inside our bedroom. Initially I used this story to show how the incivilities of life in France crept even into my sleep. I believe it also illustrates the personal dynamics of everyday village life, where people claim (or extend) their space by their behaviors, testing just how far they can go before a limit is set. It is a strange interpretation of liberty where individual *liberté* seems to trump mutual respect, and one must be on constant guard to assure to protect personal space. The everyday environment created by such *liberté* creates a vigilante spirit. When Linda and I remember this story, we have different points-of-view. She focuses on the budding solidarity; the unexpected assistance I received from two neighbors as I stood in the street, and the success of the intervention. I do not wish to diminish the success. I enjoyed the success and celebrated it for the several quiet nights that followed. But, for me, a focus on a moment of success is too narrow. It fails to acknowledge that this was the account of only one such battle. Similarly, others preceded it, and there were more still to come. These intrusions were not exceptions to the rule: these were the rule of life. It is important to understand that this prevailing norm creates "a way of life". In this environment, looking at the bright side is like expecting a plant to flourish because there has been a sunny day. Without noticing the soil, the water and the other conditions that are necessary for it to flourish. So, I began to ask myself. "Do I want to be planted here?"

A re-reading of M. Scott Peck's book *People of the Lie* was helpful to me. Peck's book makes an important statement about human behaviors that affect the quality of our lives individually, and within communities. The darker side of life is a part of life in France which I have come to know, and for which I was not prepared. Early on in our first encounters with deception, I made an entry in our journal. I repeat a section of that journal entry here:

> ...On the surface, the effort it takes to correct errors, oversights, miscommunications, and just plain shoddy workmanship was obvious to me. But in the absence of a better alternative I tolerated this unsatisfactory relationship. But in today's confrontation it became clear that we have let ourselves be used. About myself I learned - or rather was reminded – of a lesson in surrendering in the face of evil. I would and still am more likely to rise to the challenge of some injustice rather than to move out of harm's way. Your comments, my love, were so on target. They remind me of Scott Peck's *People of The Lie*. I believe we took a step today to move out of harm's way, to let it pass over rather than use any more valuable time and energy. Still I have difficulty in this yielding, but maybe tomorrow I will be one day more mature to surrender rather than to enter a power struggle with the lie that comes to steal away my life – or the life I came to France to live.

I repeat this entry here because it presents a conflict of strategies with which I still struggle. Living in France has called into question the value of having a single strategy, that of yielding, surrendering, moving out of harm's way. I believe that there is a place for both and sometimes a need for an active strategy of confrontation in the face of some behaviors. Perhaps the word "evil" is too laden with a history of judgment and not a politically correct term for these behaviors. Nevertheless, what is the name for a group of behaviors that erode basic trust among people, take what rightfully belongs to another, and distort the congruency between what we believe and say and do? I struggle with how to name it.

Some would argue that the behaviors that I describe above could, and do happen, elsewhere in the world. I would not disagree. However, I find that such an argument is a poor defense for these practices and it overlooks its effect of on the quality of life (anywhere). More to the point of this story, there appear to be no sanctions (or perhaps I should say, there are no sanctions which are effectively employed) to discourage these behaviors. Deception in everyday life is more grievous an oversight in the south of France which boasts of its quality of life. The expectation might be somewhat different if one were to choose to settle in a "Banana Republic" known for corruption and chicanery. But France sees itself and promotes itself as among the world's leaders and among the best. There is no "warning label", nor does one expect one, on pictures painted of life in the south of France.

I admit that, in retrospect, I, like most who picture their life in France, had a touch of romanticism about my hopes for living a French country life. My images of "good country folk" stirred up pictures of simplicity in its best sense, down to earth honesty, and a gentle way of life. This image is fostered frequently by all who love France and idealize this way of life. It is easy to see French country living as "pretty as a picture". However, it is an incomplete picture focused on the bright light, a glare that obscures the shadows.

I sometimes hear Francophiles categorize two types of foreigners who live in France: "Those who love France" and "Those who love to hate it". I do not share this simple dualism. And I do not see myself in this latter category. Like any dualistic view of the world, it is overly simple. I believe that it is no flaw to look at the shadow side to get a fully developed picture. None of us (no one and no one country) are as beautiful or glamorous as we think we are – or -- as the travel literature would have us believe.

I sometimes remind myself that in the broadest view of world affairs, this revelation of the shadow side of life in France falls, perhaps, near the bottom of a long list of more tragic assaults, offenses, and problems in our global village. And I sometimes find myself trying to revamp my horizons to overlook the everyday, and focus on a broader landscape. But one must compare apples to apples. I have yet to see any books on France promoting life in the south of France as a remedy for global warming, world hunger or terrorism. No, one comes to the south of France to live the celebrated French *joie de vivre*. Certainly, there are grand causes and greater world problems, but I have chosen to compare the *la vie en France*, the life we came to live, with the life in rural France that greeted us and greets us on our everyday horizon.

Throughout the writing of this book, and often in living the experiences which I have recounted, a tale from childhood returned to me. The story of "The Emperor's New Clothes" is best known for its northern European adaptation in the tales of Hans Christian Andersen. But it has its origins in the stories of Don Juan Manuel in thirteenth century Spain. I have found parallels of this story in several of the eastern countries and in English tales, but I have not been able to find a French tale with this message.

There have been many versions over time, but this brief rendition is sufficient to make the point:

Once upon a time, as all great tales begin, there lived an emperor who was quite an unremarkable fairy tale ruler. He was, it is said, quite average and gathered around him in his court quite ordinary ministers. But he had a fondness for wearing fine clothing as a sign of his importance. One day he heard that two unusual tailors, said to make the finest suit of clothes from the most beautiful cloth, had come to his kingdom. This cloth, said the tailors, had a very special quality. For, only persons most intelligent and most capable would be able to appreciate its splendor. It was invisible to anyone who was dull witted or not fit for his position. The emperor commissioned these unusual tailors to make for him the finest of clothes for his wardrobe.

After much delay and much fine living at the emperor's expense, the tailors announced that the wardrobe was complete. Being a bit nervous about whether he himself would be able to see the cloth, the emperor first sent two of his trusted men to view these new clothes. Of course, neither would admit that they could not see the cloth, and so praised it, for they feared they would be discovered to be unfit for their positions.

The new clothes were presented to the emperor. The emperor, himself fearful that he might be unmasked as dim witted and unsuited for his position, did not admit that he could not see his new wardrobe. Afraid that his ministers would think that he was stupid, he allowed the tailors to dress him for a grand state occasion and procession through town.

The emperor's new clothes were the talk of the town for all the townspeople had heard of the special commission. Everyone lined the city streets to await the procession. Secretly, they were eager to learn who among their neighbors were incompetent and ignorant.

Caught in their own bewilderment, all the townspeople wildly praised the magnificent clothes of the emperor, afraid to admit that they too could not see them.

There was a boy in the crowd, too small to see above all the others. But when raised up on his father's shoulders to see the sight at which everyone marveled, he exclaimed "The Emperor has no clothes on at all!"

At first it was hushed, and then whispered from person to person until everyone in the crowd knew that the child was right. The emperor was wearing nothing at all. Be sure that the emperor heard it and felt that they were correct, but held his head high and finished the procession still not admitting what everyone knew. He carried himself even more proudly, and the chamberlains walked along behind carrying the train that wasn't there.

The amazing tailors escaped during the procession, taking with them the wealth from this extraordinary commission.

Perhaps in telling this story of our first three years of life in France I am a voice in the crowd of popular contemporary literature on French Life, on Retirement and International Living, on Living and Working in France, and all the books that line the shelves of book sellers that sing the praises of la *vie en France*. Much of what is said of the celebrated way of life in France, is true. There is much more that is simply not said, or not heard beyond the romanticized notions of France populist marketing for tourism. Life in the south of France is a life filled with a bright sun and long shadows.

# Annotated Bibliography

Some of the books below helped form our impressions what life in France might be. Others helped us create our dreams of what we hoped life in France would be. Still others were read long before we considered life in France. They helped form our life together in Chicago, and still do today. This is the "short list" of those that were, for us, outstanding and cannot begin to include all the readings that we turned to understand French life and life in general. We are happy to share it with you. The brief notations are subjective.:

Adamson Taylor, Sally. *Culture Shock.* Portland, Oregon: Graphic Arts Center Publishing Company, Rev&Expand edition © 2003. Touches on the emotional journey and pain of leaving everything familiar to enter an unfamiliar world.

Darnton, Robert, *The Great Cat Massacre: And Other Episodes in French Cultural History.* Toronto, Canada: Random House of Canada Limited, ©1984

In places it reads like a detective story, but it is a well-documented cultural history of French folk tales and French ways of life.

Goodman, Richard. *French Dirt: The Story of a Garden in The South of France.* New York: Harper Perennial, © 1991.

Unlike others who write about the experience of living in France he gets to the soul of the experience.

Hallie, Philip, *Lest Innocent Blood Be Shed: The Story of The Village of Le Chambon And How Goodness Happened There.* New York, New York: HarperCollins Publishers Inc. ©1979

A beautiful, true story about ordinary people during extraordinary times of the Second World War. It is an affirmation that goodness can prevail in the face inhumanity and insanity. It is also an insight into the dynamics of French village life in the 20th century.

Moore, Thomas, *Care of the Soul: A Guide for Cultivating Depth and Sacredness in Everyday Life*. New York, New York: HarperCollins Publishers ©1992

In some ways this book has nothing to do with France. But it has everything to do with us, how we live our life, and the environment of our home. It gives words to a quality and way of life we saw in ourselves. The environment and hospitality of le petit jardin de l'âme B&B, is our way of sharing that life with others.

Nadeau, Jean-Benoît & Julie Barlow, *Sixty Million Frenchmen Can't Be Wrong, (why we love france but not the french)*. Naperville, Illinois: Sourcebooks Inc. ©2003

Chapter 5 The Art of Eloquence, Chapter 7 World War II: The Unforgotten War, Chapter 8 Algeria: The Unacknowledged War, Chapter 9 The Penchant for Absolutism, Chapter 12 Strong Language -- are good background to understanding contemporary French people. These chapters are researched well in each area. In other chapters, I believe it suffers from the typical explanation of French culture that tends to defend or justify French Behavior rather than shed light upon it.

Peck, M. Scott. *People of The Lie*. New York: Simon & Schuster, ©1983

This book received less publicity than his other titles concerning spiritual and mental health. But it is among the "must reads" for understanding the everyday deceits upon which some lives are built. Such self-deceptions can be personal, organizational, or cultural. It is an interesting view of how evil can become an unconscious way of life seen in everyday behaviors.

Peck, M. Scott. *A World Waiting to Be Born: Civility Rediscovered*. New York: Bantam Books, ©1994

The analogy of marriage as a monastery of two was particularly interesting for us. But the overall spiritual and psychological insight regarding incivility as a contemporary illness is significant. By incivility, Dr. Peck means conduct far more serious than a want of politeness. He sheds light on morally destructive patterns of self-absorption, callousness, and manipulativeness so ingrained in routine behavior that we often do not recognize them.

De Tocqueville, Alexis, *The Old Regime and the French Revolution*. translated by Stuart Gilbert. New York: Anchor Books Doubleday, © 1955, 1983

Although not current history, for those who take the time to read it, this book is very helpful in understanding a critical period in French history in a much different way than is popularly understood. It forms a necessary historical framework for understanding France today.

Zeldin, Theodore, *The French*. London: William Collins Sons & Co. Ltd. Also, Collins Harvill and The Harvill Press. ©1983

This is a tombe and slow reading, often cited by others as reference. To counter stereotypes of the French and French ways, he errs in presenting such a varied description of French ways as to have no distinguishing characteristics. Are the French so much like everyone else?

There are two general categories of literature on France which are significant. These two general topics are important, rather than any one book:

• I have passed over the many accounts of history and fiction and biographies related to the Cathares. These are great reading to understand the historical background of the Midi region and why it is different from the rest of France. Many have worthwhile insights into what has shaped the Languedoc and the Occitans.
• I have not listed the numerous light readings of contemporary French culture found in the travel literature section of bookstores. We enjoyed many of them. As a genre they are sometimes helpful, not infallible, and most often written from the perspective of someone who has spent most of their French life in Paris. Using Paris as a frame of reference is often not helpful for understanding the south of France.

www.ingramcontent.com/pod-product-compliance
Lightning Source LLC
Chambersburg PA
CBHW071501080526
44587CB00014B/2180